The Countess de Segur

Sophie's troubles

The Countess de Segur

Sophie's troubles

ISBN/EAN: 9783741135224

Manufactured in Europe, USA, Canada, Australia, Japa

Cover: Foto ©Andreas Hilbeck / pixelio.de

Manufactured and distributed by brebook publishing software (www.brebook.com)

The Countess de Segur

Sophie's troubles

Sophie's Troubles,

FORTY-EIGHT ILLUSTRATIONS.

—BY—

The Countess de Ségur.
Née Rostopchine.

Translated by P. P. S.

P. J. KENEDY & SONS

New York and Philadelphia

TABLE OF CONTENTS.

		Page
I.	The Wax Doll	5
II.	The Funeral	17
III.	The Lime	23
IV.	The Little Fishes	31
V.	The Black Chicken	43
VI.	The Bee	51
VII.	The Wet Head	59
VIII.	The Clipped Eyebrows	69
IX.	The Horses' Bread	75
X.	The Cream and Warm Bread	85
XI.	The Squirrel	95
XII.	The Tea	113
XIII.	The Wolves	131
XIV.	The Scratched Cheek	143
XV.	Elizabeth	155
XVI.	The Conserved Fruits	161
XVII.	The Cat and the Bullfinch	165
XVIII.	The Work-box	203
XIX.	The Donkey	217
XX.	The Little Carriage	251
XXI.	The Tortoise	269
XXII.	The Departure	283

TO
MY GRANDDAUGHTER, ELIZABETH FRESNEAU.

DEAR CHILD, you often say to me: "O grandmother, how I love you, you are so good!" Grandmother was not always good; and there are many other children who were as bad as she, and who, like herself, corrected their faults.

The following is the true story of a little girl, with whom your grandmother was intimately acquainted in childhood. This little girl was ill-tempered, but she became gentle; she was a glutton, but she became temperate; she was untruthful, but she became sincere; she was dishonest, but she became honest; in fine, she was a very bad little girl, but she became good. Grandmother tried to do likewise. Follow her example, my dear little children; the task will not be such a difficult one to you who have not so many and great faults to correct as Sophie had.

COUNTESS DE SEGUR,
née Rostopchine.

L.

The Wax Doll.

"OH, nurse, nurse," exclaimed Sophie, running into her room one day, "come quick and open this box papa has sent me from Paris. I believe there is a wax doll in it, for he promised me one."

NURSE.

Where is the box?

SOPHIE.

In the hall; please, nurse, come as fast as you can.

The nurse put down her work, and followed Sophie into the hall. A white wooden box was on a chair, and as the nurse opened it, Sophie descried the light curly hair of a wax doll. She uttered a cry of joy, and attempted to seize the doll still enveloped in its paper wrappings.

NURSE.

Take care! don't pull it out yet, you will break it; it is tied in with strings.

SOPHIE.

Break them, pull them off, quick, nurse, so I may get my doll.

Instead of jerking at and pulling the strings, the nurse cut them with her scissors; she then unwrapped the papers, and Sophie clasped to her heart the most beautiful wax doll she had ever seen. Its rosy cheeks were dimpled, its eyes a bright blue, and its waxen neck, breast, and arms, plump and charming. Its dress was very simple, being merely a robe of festooned percale, a blue sash, cotton stockings, and high boots of black glazed leather.

Sophie embraced it in raptures of delight many times, and, holding it in her arms, she began to caper about the room. Her cries of joy attracted the attention of her cousin, Paul, a little boy, five years of age, who was on a visit to her.

"O, Paul! look at this beautiful doll papa has sent me!" she exclaimed.

PAUL.

Give it to me, so that I can see it better.

SOPHIE.

No, you will break it.

PAUL.

I promise you I will be very careful; I will give it back to you immediately.

Sophie handed her cousin the doll, still cautioning him not to let it fall. Paul took it, and, after a careful scrutinizing, returned it to her, shaking his head.

SOPHIE.

Why do you shake your head?

PAUL.

Because this doll is not solid; I am afraid you will break it.

SOPHIE.

Oh! don't worry about that, I am going to take such care of it, that I shall never break it. I am going to ask mamma to invite Camille and Madeleine to breakfast with us, so that they, too, may see my pretty doll.

PAUL.

They will break it for you.

SOPHIE.

Oh, no! they are too fond of me to pain me by breaking my dear doll.

Next morning, Sophie combed and dressed her doll in readiness to receive her friends. She thought, whilst dressing it, that the doll looked pale.

"Perhaps she is cold," said Sophie, "her feet feel frozen. I will put her in the sun a little while, so that my friends may see I take good care of her, and keep her warm and comfortable."

And with these words, she went towards the window to lay her doll in the sun.

"What are you doing at the window, Sophie?" inquired her mamma.

SOPHIE.

I am warming my doll, mamma, she is very cold.

MAMMA.

Take care, or she will melt.

SOPHIE.

Oh! no, mamma, there is no danger; she is as hard as wood.

MAMMA.

But the heat will soften her; I warn you now, lest you do her some mischief.

Sophie would not listen to her mamma, but laid her doll full length in the broiling sun.

At that instant, she heard the noise of a carriage; her little friends had arrived, and she ran to meet them. Paul had met them at the entrance, and they ran into the room, all talking at once. Nothwithstanding their impatience to see the doll, they stopped to say good morning to Mme. De Réan, Sophie's mamma; after which, they followed Sophie, who, picking up the doll, regarded it with consternation.

"The doll is blind, she has no eyes," said Madeleine.

CAMILLE.

What a pity! how pretty she is!

MADELEINE.

But what made her blind? she must have had eyes.

Sophie said nothing, but looked at her doll and wept.

MME. DE RÉAN.

I warned you, Sophie, not to lay your doll in the sun, yet you persisted in doing it. Fortunately, her face and arms have not had time to melt. Come now, don't cry any more, I am a very skilful doctor, and perhaps I can restore her eyes.

"It's impossible, mamma," said Sophie, weeping, "her eyes are gone."

Smiling, Mme. De Réan took the doll and gave it a little shake; something rattled in its head. "Those are the eyes, making that noise in the head," said she, "the wax has melted around them and they have fallen in. I think I can get them out. Undress the doll, children, whilst I prepare my instruments."

Immediately, Paul and the three little girls rushed at the doll to undress it. Sophie dried her tears, and impatiently awaited the result of her mother's attempts to restore its eyes.

Mme. De Réan returned, and cut with her scissors the stitches fastening the doll's head to the body. Its eyes which were in the head fell out upon her knees. She took them up

The eyes which were in its head fall out on her lap. (Page 10.)

with pincers, replaced them in the cavities, and
then to prevent their falling out again, she
poured in the head, just around the sockets of
the eye, some melted wax she had brought in
a little saucepan. Waiting a few minutes till
the wax had hardened, she sewed the head on
to the body again.

Meanwhile the little ones had not budged.
Sophie with trembling heart, watched all the
proceedings, very dubious of their success;
and when she saw her doll restored to its
former beauty she threw her arms around her
mother's neck and loaded her with caresses.

"Thanks, thanks, dear mamma," she cried,
"another time I will certainly listen to you."

The doll was soon dressed again, and seated
on a little armchair which the children carried
about in triumph, singing the praises of Mme.
De Réan's skill in the following lines:

"O dear mamma! O dear mamma!
Let showers of kisses speak
Our love for her, that angel good—
Kisses upon her precious cheek."

For a long time after this, the doll was well
cared for and much loved; but gradually, her

charms disappeared, as the following anecdotes will show.

One day, thinking her doll ought to be washed because children were always washed, Sophie took water, a sponge and soap, and set about the operation, which succeeded so well, that all the color was washed out of the doll's face, its lips and cheeks becoming as white as if it were ill, and remaining thus. Sophie wept, but it did not restore her doll's color.

Another day, wishing to curl its hair, she put it up in papers, and then pinched them with a warm iron. But alas! when the papers were removed, the hair came off also,—the iron was too hot, Sophie had burnt all the hair off her doll's head, and now quite bald, it was a pitiable looking little object indeed. Sophie wept, but the doll remained bald.

Another time, greatly engrossed with the education of her doll, Sophie wished to teach it to whirl around. She held it up by a cord tied to its arms; and the poor doll not being well fastened, fell and broke an arm. Mme. de Réan tried to mend it, but as the pieces were wanting, and she had to use up much of the wax of its substance in heating it, one arm remained shorter than the other. Sophie wept, but the arm remained shorter.

Again, deeming a foot bath beneficial to her doll's health, as it was customary for grown persons to take foot baths, Sophie poured some boiling water in a little bucket, into which she

plunged her doll's feet. On withdrawing the doll, its feet had melted and were in the bucket. Sophie wept, but the doll remained without feet.

After so many accidents, Sophie lost all affection for her doll, which had now become frightful, and an object of ridicule to her friends. At last, one day, in trying to teach it to climb a tree she held it up to a branch and seated it there; but not being secure in its position, it fell, its head striking against the stones, and breaking into a hundred pieces. Sophie did not weep this time, but invited her friends to the doll's funeral.

II.

The Funeral.

CAMILLE and Madeleine receiving their invitations, came to the doll's funeral; they were delighted, nor were Sophie and Paul less so.

SOPHIE.

Come quick, we are waiting for you to help make the doll's coffin.

CAMILLE.

Of what shall we make it?

SOPHIE.

Of an old toy box I had, that nurse has covered with pink percale; it looks very pretty—come see it.

The children ran to the room where the nurse was just finishing the pillow and mattress for the box; it was such a charming coffin they admired it exceedingly. The doll was placed in it, its crushed head, melted feet and broken arm concealed by a coverlet of pink silk.

The box was now put on a litter which Sophie's mamma had made for the purpose. Of course, they all wished to carry it, but as this was impossible since there was room for two only, it was agreed, after some pushing and disputing, that Sophie and Paul, the two smallest should carry the bier, whilst Camille and Madeleine should walk, the one before, the other behind, bearing a basket of flowers and leaves to scatter over the grave.

The procession reaching Sophie's little garden, they set down the litter with the box containing the remains of the unfortunate doll, and began to dig the grave, into which when deep enough, they lowered the coffin, covered it with flowers and leaves, then replaced the earth, and as promptly planted on the spot two lilacs. As a finishing touch to the interment, they ran to the kitchen-garden pond and filled their little watering-pots to water the lilacs. This was the occasion of renewed sports and mirth, as they pursued one another with the watering-pot, running and laughing,

They plant two Lilac bushes. (Page 18.)

whilst trying to escape a sprinkling. Such a lively funeral was never before witnessed. To be sure, the deceased was only an old doll, colorless, bald, without legs or head, and neither loved nor regretted by any one. The day ended gayly, and when Camille and Madeleine said good-bye, they advised Paul and Sophie to break another doll, so as to afford them a repetition of that day's interesting and amusing interment.

III.

The Lime.

LITTLE Sophie was not obedient. Her mamma had forbidden her going alone into the yard where the masons were building a house for the chickens, the pea fowls and the guinea hens. As Sophie liked to see the masons at work, whenever her mamma went where they were, she took Sophie, but always kept her within reach. Sophie however, preferred running about at random, and, one day, said to her mother.

"Mamma, why do you forbid my going to see the masons without you? and when I am with you, why do you keep me always at your side."

MAMMA.

Because it is dangerous for you to be in the way of the stones and bricks which the masons are handling; you might also slip on the sand, or get injured by the lime they have to use.

SOPHIE.

Oh! mamma, I would be very careful, and besides, the sand and lime can't do me any harm.

MAMMA.

You think so because you are a little girl, but I who am much older know that lime burns.

SOPHIE.

But mamma :—
"See here, Sophie," said her mother interrupting her, "don't argue any more, but be quiet; I know much better than you what will hurt you and what will not, and I forbid your going into the yard without me."

Sophie hung her head and made no reply, but frowning said to herself:

"I will go for all that; it amuses me, and I am going."

It was not long before she had an opportunity of putting her disobedient resolution into

practice. In the course of the next hour, the gardener came for Mme. De Rean to select some geraniums she had intended buying, and Sophie was left alone. Looking carefully around to see whether the nurse or chamber-

maid were within sight, and perceiving that they were not, she ran to the door, opened it, and went into the yard. The masons continued their work never giving a thought to Sophie, who went all about, seeing and examining everything. Her attention was arrested by the sight of a great basin of lime, white and smooth as cream.

Oh! how white and pretty this is!" said she, "this is the first time that I have had a

good look at it, for mamma would never let me go near it. How smooth it is! It must be very soft and agreeable under foot, I am going to slide all over it, just as if it were ice."

And Sophie steps one foot upon the lime believing it firm and solid like the ground. But her foot sinks, and to prevent falling, she must needs put forward the other, only to find herself sinking in the lime up to her knees. She screams in terror, and a mason running to her, lifts her out, and places her on the ground.

"Take off your shoes and stockings as quick as possible, Miss," he says, "they are already burnt, and if you keep them on, the lime will burn your legs too."

Sophie looks at her legs, and sees that though covered with lime, her shoes and stockings are as black as if they had been in the fire. She screams louder than ever, particularly as she begins to feel the lime burning her legs. Happily the nurse is not far off, and running to the rescue, perceives immediately what has happened. Snatching off Sophie's shoes and stockings, she wipes the little feet and legs upon her own apron, picks Sophie up, and carries her to the house. At the very moment Sophie reaches her chamber, Mme. De Réan enters it to pay the florist.

"What is the matter?" said Mme. de Réan

anxiously. "Are you sick, Sophie? Why are you bare-footed?"

Sophie, filled with shame, made no reply; but the nurse recounted all that had happened, and how narrowly Sophie had escaped having her legs burnt by the lime.

"If I had not been very near the yard, and gone instantly, her legs would have been burnt like my apron," said the nurse, "and Madame can see how it looks; it is full of holes."

Mme. de Réan saw indeed, that the apron was nearly destroyed. Turning to Sophie, she said:

"I ought to whip you, Miss, for your disobedience, but the good God has already punished you by the fright you have had; so, I shall give you no other punishment than that of buying nurse a new apron with the five franc piece in your purse, which you had put away for the village festival."

In vain did Sophie weep and implore her mother not to take the five franc piece; mamma was inexorable, and Sophie, with good reason, resolved that another time, she would listen to her, and not venture on forbidden ground.

IV.

THE LITTLE FISHES.

SOPHIE was thoughtless and often did a great deal of mischief from not stopping to think.

Listen to the following account of one of her tricks:

Her mother had some little fishes not longer than a pin, and no thicker than the quill of a pigeon's feather. Mme. De Réan was very fond of these little fishes which she kept in a vessel of water, the bottom covered with sand, in which they could bury and conceal themselves at will. Every day, she fed them on bread; and it was great amusement for Sophie to watch them dart after the crumbs, and dispute with one another for them.

One day, Sophie's papa gave her a pretty little tortoise-shell knife. She was delighted, and always used it for cutting her bread, apples, biscuit, flowers, etc.

One morning she was playing; the nurse had given her some bread which she cut in little pieces, some almonds that she also sliced and some salad leaves. She now asked the nurse for oil and vinegar to make salad.

"No;" said the nurse, "I will cheerfully give you salad, but not oil and vinegar to soil your clothes."

After sprinkling her salad leaves with salt, Sophie still had a great deal of the latter left.

"If I only had something to salt" said she, "I dont wish to salt my bread, I must have either meat or fish—Oh; what a splendid idea; I will salt mamma's fishes; some, I will cut in pieces with my little knife, others, I will salt whole. How amusing that will be, and what a nice dish they will make!"

And never reflecting one instant on the mischief she would work, depriving her mother of the pet fishes so prized, or, how the poor little things would suffer from being salted alive or cut in pieces, Sophie runs into the room where they are and approaching the vessel, fishes them all up out of the water, puts them in one of her dishes, and returns to her little table. She now spreads them out on a plate. But the poor little creatures feeling ill at ease out of the water, struggle and flop about most uncomfortably. To quiet them, Sophie sprinkles them all with salt, upon the head, back,

and tail; and very soon they cease to struggle, they are dead! When her plate was filled thus, she took more of them, and began to cut them in pieces. At the first gash of the knife, the poor fishes writhed in pain, but they likewise soon became motionless for they too were dead. After cutting up the second one, Sophie perceived that she had killed them. She now looked at the salted fish, and seeing that they did not move, she examined them attentively only to discover to her consternation that they also were dead. At this her face became as red as a cherry.

"What will mamma say?" she said to herself. "What will become of me, poor wretch! How shall I conceal this from mamma?"

After a moments reflection her countenance brightened—she had, according to her own judgment, devised a most excellent means of deceiving her mother.

Quickly collecting both the salted and the cut up fishes, she put them in a little dish, steals softly out of the room and stealthily replaces them in their vessel of water.

"Mamma," says she to herself, "will think they have killed one another fighting among themselves. I must now wipe off my dishes and knife and puts the salt away. Fortunately, nurse does not know that I have been where the fishes were, as she was busy with her work and not thinking about me." Sophie noise-

lessly returns to her room, seats herself at
the little table again, and continues her play.
Soon she arises, gets a book and begins to look
at the pictures. But the pictures fail to inter-
est her,—she is ill at ease, and in constant
dread of seeing her mother enter the room.

Suddenly, Sophie starts nervously and
blushes,—she hears the voice of Mme. De Réan
summoning the servants in a tone of severity
and displeasure, she hears the servants come
and go, and she trembles lest the next person
called should be the nurse or herself; but the
talking ceases and all becomes quiet.

The nurse, who likewise hears the noise and
is curious as to the cause, puts down her work
and leaves the room.

In a quarter of an hour she returns.

"How fortunate for us," said she to Sophie,
"that we have both been in our room all the
while! Just imagine, your mamma went to
see the fishes and found them all dead, some
whole, and others cut in pieces! She has questioned all the servants as to who could have
killed the poor little creatures, but no one can
or will tell anything about it. I have just seen
your mother, and she asked me if you had

been where the fishes were. Luckily, I could say that you had not budged from this room where you had been playing dinner. 'It is singular;' said your mamma, 'I would have laid a wager that Sophie was the author of this mischief' 'Oh! Madame,' I answered, 'Sophie would never be guilty of such cruelty.' 'So much the better,' said your mamma, 'for I should have punished her severely. It is lucky for her that you assure me, she has not left her room, and that consequently, she could not have killed my poor fishes.' 'Oh! Madame, 'I am sure she did not,' said I.''

Sophie made no reply, but remained motionless with her head cast down, her cheeks a bright red, and her eyes filled with tears. For an instant, she thought of confessing the deed and telling nurse who had wrought so much mischief, but her courage failed her. Seeing her thus, nurse mistook her confusion for grief, at the fishes' death.

"I knew," said the nurse, "that you would be as much distressed as your mother at what has happened to these poor little creatures. But be consoled; they were not happy in their prison, for the bowl was only a prison to

Madame Rean called all the servants. (Page 35).

them; now, they are dead and their sufferings are over. Don't think of them any more, but come let me prepare you for dinner, it is nearly ready."

Sophie was washed and had her hair combed without uttering a word. When she entered the dining-room her mother was there.

Sophie," said she, " has nurse told you what has befallen my little fishes?"

SOPHIE.

Yes, mamma.

MADAME DE RÉAN.

If nurse had not assured me that you were in your room with her, the whole time after leaving me, I should have charged you with the deed; all the servants positively deny it. But I believe that Simon who took care of the fishes, changing the water and sand every morning was the one who killed them—it was to rid himself of the trouble they gave him, so, I shall discharge him to-morrow.

SOPHIE, (*frightened*).

Oh! mamma the poor man! What will become of his wife and children?

MADAME DE RÉAN.

So much the worse for him; he ought not to have killed my little fishes that had never done him any harm! Just think how he made them suffer, cutting them in pieces!

SOPHIE.

But it was not he, mamma, who killed them! I assure you it was not!

MADAME DE RÉAN.

How do you know it was not? I believe it was he; it could have been no one else, and to-morrow, I shall send him away.

Sophie, bursting into tears and clasping her hands, cried out:

"Oh, no! mamma, don't send him away. It was I who took the little fishes and killed them."

"You!" exclaimed Mme. De Réan in surprise, "what nonsense! you who were so fond of the little creatures! you tortured and killed them! I see that you say this to excuse Simon."

"No, mamma," answered Sophie; "I assure you it was I! yes, it was I! I didn't intend to kill them; I wished only to salt them, and I thought salt would do them no harm. And when I cut them in pieces, I didn't know it hurt them, because they didn't cry. When I found they were dead, I took them back to the vessel of water, and nurse, who was at her work, didn't miss me when I went or came."

For a few moments, Mme. De Réan was mute with astonishment at Sophie's confession; and when the latter timidly raised her eyes, she encountered those of her mother fixed upon her, but without the slightest expression of anger or severity.

"Sophie," said Mme. De Réan at last, "if I had learned by chance, or rather providentially I should say, what you have just told me, I should have punished you most severely. But the good spirit you have shown in confessing your fault, to exonerate Simon, insures your pardon; so I shall not reproach you, for I am sure you feel most sensibly how cruel you have been to the poor little fishes, in not reflecting both that the salt must kill them, and also, that it would be impossible to cut in pieces and kill any creature whatever without inflicting suffering."

And, seeing that Sophie wept bitterly, she added:

"Don't cry any more, Sophie; but never forget that to obtain pardon for our faults, we must confess them."

Sophie dried her tears, and thanked her mother; but all that day she remained very sad at the thought of having killed her little friends, the fishes.

V.

THE BLACK CHICKEN.

MME. De Réan had some hens sitting on eggs, from which she expected to hatch a species of chicken with superb crests; and every day she went to the poultry yard to see if the eggs had hatched, accompanied by Sophie, who carried a little basket of bread which she crumbled and threw to the chickens. As soon as she made her appearance, they all flocked around her, picking at the bread in her hands and basket, Sophie laughing and running, and the chickens following, much to her amusement.

Meanwhile, her mother went into a fine, large covered shed, where the sitting hens were lodged like princesses, and indeed better cared for than many princesses. When all the bread had been dispensed, Sophie rejoined her mother, and looked at the little chickens just out of their shells, and too young to be let run about with the larger poultry. One morning, on entering the hen house, Sophie perceived that her mother held in her hands a magnificent chicken, not more than an hour old.

SOPHIE.

Oh, mamma! the pretty chicken! his feathers are as black as a crow's.

MADAME DE RÉAN.

Yes, and look at this beautiful top-knot; he will be magnificent.

Mme. de Réan replaced him under the sitting hen. Scarcely had she done so, when the hen gave the poor chicken a hard peck with her bill. Mme. De Réan retaliated with a tap on the cruel hen, and picking up the little chicken which had fallen over with a cry of pain, she placed it again with the hen. This time, the furious creature pecked it smartly two or three times, and ran at it whenever it made an attempt to come near her.

Mme. De Réan, hastening to pick it up, lest the unnatural mother should peck it to death, gave it a drop of water to revive it.

"What shall we do with this little chicken?" said she; "if we leave it with the wicked mother she will kill it, and it is so beautiful I should like very much to raise it."

SOPHIE.

Oh! listen to me, mamma: let us put it in a big basket in the room where my playthings are; we can keep it there, and feed it until it is big enough to go back to the hen house.

MADAME DE RÉAN.

I believe you are right; put it in your bread-basket, and let us fix it a bed.

SOPHIE.

Oh, mamma! look at its neck! it is bleeding, and its back, too.

MADAME DE RÉAN.

Those places are where the hen pecked it; when you take it to the house, ask the nurse for some ointment to put on its wounds.

Sophie was not pleased that the poor chicken had been hurt, but she certainly was delighted to have an occasion of applying the remedy. So, running into the house ahead of her mother, she showed the nurse the chicken, and asking for the ointment, immediately applied a little of it to every spot that was bleeding. Then she prepared a mixture of egg, bread, and milk, which she stirred and crushed for an hour. But the chicken was suffering, and had no desire to eat; it would only drink a few drops of fresh water.

In about three days its wounds were healed, and it was walking around the door leading to the garden. One month later, it had grown so rapidly and improved to such a degree, that one might readily have supposed it two months older than it really was. It was now remarkably beautiful, its feathers a very rare blue black, smooth and glossy as if just dipped in water; its head ornamented with an enormous crest of mingled black, orange, blue, red and white; its bill and feet pink, its eyes bright and sparkling, and its gait firm and proud,—seldom did one see so handsome a chicken.

It was Sophie who had charge of it, she who fed it, and watched it whilst it got the fresh air in front of the house. In a few days, it was to be transferred to the poultry yard, because it had grown beyond her management; for sometimes she would chase it half an hour and then not succeed in catching it; and once, it came near being drowned in a little pool of water that it missed seeing, in trying to escape her.

She endeavored to prevent its straying out of reach by tying a ribbon to its foot, and holding it thus; but it struggled so violently that she was obliged to remove the ribbon, lest it break its leg. Her mamma then forbade her taking it from the poultry yard.

"There are so many hawks about here, they

might carry it off; we must wait till it is grown before letting it loose," said Mme. De Réan.

But Sophie who was not always obedient, continued to let her chicken out, unknown to her mother; and, one day, seeing that her mother was busy writing, she took advantage of the opportunity to bring him around in front of the house, where he could amuse himself seeking gnats and worms in the sand and

grass. Not many steps off, Sophie sat combing her doll's hair, frequently glancing up to see that her chicken did not stray off. Raising her eyes as usual, she now saw with astonishment a big bird with a crooked beak, alight not three steps from the chicken, which it regarded with an air of ferocity, at the same time, glancing timidly at herself. The chicken did not budge—it trembled and crouched to the ground.

"What a queer bird," said Sophie, "He is handsome, but he acts so strangely; when he looks at me he seems afraid, and when he looks at the chicken, his eyes are furious! Ha! ha! ha! how funny he is!"

At that instant, with a piercing, savage shriek, the bird darting upon the chicken

which responded by a plaintive cry, seized him in its claws and flew off at full speed.

Sophie was speechless with astonishment. Her mamma running at the sound of the bird, inquired of her what had happened, and Sophie replied that a bird has carried off the chicken, and she could not imagine what it meant.

"It means," said her mother, "that you are a disobedient little girl, that the bird is a hawk, which you have let carry off and devour my beautiful chicken; and that you may go to your room, where you will dine and remain till evening; and perhaps this may teach you to be more obedient another time."

Sophie hung her head and walked sadly to her room where she dined on soup and a dish of meat, brought her by the nurse who was tenderly attached to her little charge. Sophie shed many tears over the death of her chicken, the loss of which she mourned a long time.

V.

THE BEE.

SOPHIE and her cousin Paul were one day playing in their room, amusing themselves catching the flies that crawled about over the windows. Each fly when captured was put in a little paper box Sophie's papa had made them.

When quite a number had been caught, Paul wished to see what they were doing in the box.

"Give me the box," said he to Sophie who held it, "let us see what the flies are about."

Sophie gave it to him, and they very cautiously opened it to peep in. Paul put his eye to the aperture and exclaimed:

"Ah! how funny! they are moving all about and battling with one another; here is one that has pulled off its companion's paw! Oh! what contention! some are falling down and some are getting up!"

SOPHIE'S TROUBLES.

"Let me have a look, Paul, it is my turn now," said Sophie.

Paul made no reply, but continued to peep through the aperture and recount what he saw.

Sophie became impatient, and taking a corner of the box, she drew it gently towards her; Paul did the same; Sophie got angry and pulled a little harder, Paul followed her ex-

ample; Sophie now gave such a jerk that the box came in two, and all the flies rushed out, settling themselves on the eyes, nose and cheeks of their little tormentors, who slapped and brushed away at them most vigorously.

"It is all your fault, Paul," said Sophie, "if you had been more obliging, and given me the box, it would not have been torn to pieces."

"No, it is your fault," replied Paul; "if you

had been less impatient, you would have waited a little for the box, and we should still have had it whole, instead of its being all torn like it is now."

SOPHIE.

You are selfish, and think of nobody but yourself.

PAUL.

And you—you are angry now, just like the turkeys on the farm.

SOPHIE.

I am not at all angry, Sir, but I think you a very bad, wicked boy.

PAUL.

I am not a bad, wicked boy, Miss; and it is only because I tell you the truth, that you get red with anger, just like the turkeys with their red combs.

SOPHIE.

I will not play any longer with such a bad boy as you, Sir.

PAUL.

Nor will I play any longer with a bad girl like you, Miss.

And sulking, each retired to a corner of the

room. Sophie soon grew weary of this, but, wishing to make Paul think she was enjoying herself, she set about catching flies again, singing as she did so. But there were few remaining, and these were not easily caught. Sud-

denly, she espied with joy, a big bee quietly resting in a corner of the window. Remembering that bees could sting she did not attempt to pick it up in her naked fingers, but, taking out her pocket handkerchief, she threw it over the poor bee, and thus seized it, ere it had time to save itself.

Paul, who was also weary of his monotonous corner, seeing Sophie catch the bee, said to her:

"What are you going to do with that bee?"

"Let me alone, bad boy; it is none of your business what I am going to do with it," was the rude reply.

"Pardon, pardon, Miss Furious; I, indeed, beg your pardon for having spoken to you, and for having forgotten that you were so ill-bred and impertinent."

Making a mock reverence, Sophie answered:

"I will tell mamma, Sir, that you find me ill-bred, and no doubt she will be pleased to hear it, as she raised me."

"Oh! no, Sophie," said Paul, anxiously, "don't tell her that, it would get me a scolding."

"Yes, I will tell her," she replied; "and if you are scolded, so much the better; it will please me greatly."

"Wicked thing!" was Paul's retort; "I will have nothing more to say to you!"

And Paul now turned his chair, so as not to see Sophie, who delighted at having worried and frightened him, began to occupy herself with the bee again. Cautiously lifting one corner of the handkerchief a little, she gave the bee a slight squeeze between her fingers over the handkerchief, to disable it from flying; and then took from her pocket her little knife.

"Now," said she, "I am going to cut off its head, to punish it for all the stings it has given in its life."

Suiting the action to the word, she put the poor insect on the floor, still holding it covered with the handkerchief, and with one stroke of her knife, its head was off.

Finding this quite amusing, she continued to cut it in pieces, and was so engrossed that she did not hear her mamma enter the room. Seeing Sophie kneeling, bent over, and almost motionless, Mme. de Réan approached quietly, just as the poor bee s last leg was being cut off.

A sharp and most unexpected pull of the ear apprised Sophie both of her mamma's presence and of her indignation at such an act of cruelty.

She arose instantly with a shriek, and stood trembling before her mother.

"You are a very bad, cruel girl," said the latter, "tormenting and killing this poor insect after all I said to you when you salted and killed my poor little fishes!"

SOPHIE.

Indeed, indeed, mamma, I forgot.

MME. DE RÉAN.

Well, Miss, I shall help you to remember,— first, by depriving you of your knife for a year, and also, by obliging you to wear a necklace made of the pieces of this bee, fixed on a ribbon, which necklace you will wear until it crumbles to pieces.

In vain did Sophie beg and implore her mamma not to punish her thus. Mme. De Réan paid not the least attention to her; but, calling the nurse to bring her some black ribbon, she soon prepared the dreaded necklace, and Sophie was decorated with it. Paul dared not laugh; he was mute with consternation, whilst all this was going on; but when they were left alone, touched at Sophie's mortification and grief, which vented itself in loud sobs, he ran to her side, and embracing her, begged pardon for all the unkind things he had been saying to her, and tried his utmost to convince her that, after all, her necklace was not ugly; the effect of the different colors of the bee being such as to make her collar look somewhat like one of jet and precious stones. Sophie thanked him for his sympathy which was really a great consolation, yet she could not help feeling chagrined at her new ornament. For the space of a week it remained intact; but finally, one lucky day, in playing with her, Paul handled it so roughly that the pieces of the bee were crushed, and fell off, leaving nothing but the black ribbon. He ran immediately to tell his aunt, who now permitted her little daughter to discard it. Thus was Sophie cured of a fault, for never again did she seek amusement in what gave any creature pain.

VII.

The Wet Head.

SOPHIE was a little coquette very fond of dress; and liking to be thought pretty, —and pretty, nevertheless, she was not. The following is a picture of her,—a little girl with a round, fat face of bright lively expression, having a clear, fresh complexion, very large gray eyes, a turned-up nose somewhat large, a mouth far from small and always ready to laugh, and light hair, not curly, but perfectly straight and cut short like a boy's. Although Sophie loved finery, her mother always dressed her plainly, a simple dress of white percale made low neck and short sleeves, both in summer and in winter, stockings rather coarse, and black leather shoes constituting her exterior apparel. She wore neither hat nor glove, her mamma believing it best to habituate her thus to sun, rain, wind, cold.

Sophie was especially desirous of having curly hair, having once heard much admiration bestowed upon the pretty light curls of one of her little friends, Camille De Fleurville. Since then, she had tried every way she could think of to make her own hair curl, and the following plan among others:

One afternoon it rained very hard, and was so warm that all the windows and outer doors were kept open. Sophie stood at the door for a while, not venturing out as her mamma had forbidden her; but, occasionally, she stretched forth her arm to feel the rain falling on it; next she craned her neck a little to get a few drops on her head. In doing this, she perceived that the water was running from the spout in a copious stream; and immediately, remembering that Camille's hair was always most curly when wetted,

"Oh!" she exclaimed, "if I give mine a good soaking, perhaps it will curl too!"

And running out in the rain, she stood under the spout, joyfully letting the water descend upon her head, neck, arms and back. When completely drenched, she re-entered the house, and began to wipe her head with her handker-

Sophie holds her head under the water-spout. (Page 63).

chief, taking care to rub it vigorously to
produce the desired curls. In a few moments,
the handkerchief was so wet that she must
have another, and in running to her chamber
to get it whom should she meet but mamma!
Poor Sophie, her clothing soaking, her short
wet hair standing out all over her head like
bristles, stood motionless and trembling with
fright. Mme. De Réan was astonished for
a moment, but the next, she burst out laughing, so ridiculous was the little figure before
her.

"What a bright idea must have struck you,
Miss," said she. "If you could only see yourself I am sure you could not help laughing,
just as I do! I forbade your going out, but
you have disobeyed me as usual; and now, for
a punishment, you will come to dinner in the
very trim you are in now, your clothing
drenched, your hair bristling all over your head;
and thus let your papa and your cousin Paul
become acquainted with some of your beautiful
contrivances. Take this handkerchief and
wipe your face, neck and arms."

Just as Mme. De Réan finished speaking, M.
De Réan and Paul entered. Both stood a

moment in bewildered astonishment, at sight of the poor, blushing, mortified, ridiculous little figure before them, and then burst out laughing. The more Sophie colored and hung her head, the greater her embarrassment and discomfiture, the more ridiculous was her appearance with her hair standing out upon her head, and her wet garments clinging to her. At last, M. De Réan asked what this masquerade meant, and if Sophie was going to dine in Mardi Gras costume.

MME. DE RÉAN.

It doubtless means one of her contrivances to have curly hair. She is determined, if possible, to have curls like Camille, and noticing that Camille always wets her hair to make it curl, Sophie thought she would try the same with hers.

M. DE RÉAN.

Ah! so this is the result of vanity—wishing to render herself pretty, she has succeeded in making herself a little fright.

PAUL.

Oh! my poor Sophie, do run quickly and

Her hair in disorder and her wet garments made her appear ridiculous. Page 64).

comb your hair and put on dry clothing. If you could see how funny you look, you wouldn't stay two minutes as you are.

MME. DE RÉAN.

No; she dines with us just as she is—in her beautiful coiffure and her dress soaking and covered with sand.

Paul, interrupting Mme. De Réan, said in a tone of compassion,

"Oh! aunt, please do forgive her, and let her have her hair fixed and her clothing changed."

M. DE RÉAN

And I join Paul in begging you to forgive her this time. If she repeats the offence, I will not ask you to let her off again.

SOPHIE, *(in sobs and tears).*

Indeed, papa, I promise you, I will never do so any more.

MME. DE RÉAN.

Well, Miss, to oblige your papa, I will allow you to go to your room and put on dry clothing and make yourself presentable; but you will not dine with us; you will come to the dining room when we have finished our dinner.

PAUL.

Oh! please let her dine with us, aunt.

MME. DE RÉAN.

No, Paul, ask no' more concessions; I have granted all I intend granting. Go to your room, Sophie.

Sophie dined in her chamber after being combed and dressed. When dinner was over, Paul came for her and they both went to play in the room where their playthings were kept. Sophie never stood out in the rain again to make her hair curl.

VIII.

The Clipped Eyebrows.

ANOTHER thing Sophie greatly desired to have, was heavy eyebrows. Some one had said before her one day, that little Louise De Berg would be pretty if she had eye-brows of any account. Now, Sophie's were very light in color, and very thin, so that they made not

much show. She had also heard that to strengthen and make the hair thick it must be cut often.

Looking in the glass one day, and perceiving how thin her eye-brows were, she said to herself,

"If cutting the hair makes it grow out long and thick, I don't see why cutting the eye-brows

should'nt have the same effect on them—they are hair too. I am going to try it on mine—that is just what I'll do."

And suiting the action to the word, she takes the scissors and clips her eye-brows as short as possible. Another look in the glass shows her such a ridiculous picture that she is afraid to go to the dining-room or meet any of the family.

"I'll wait until dinner is served," said she, "and no one will think of noticing me, when they are all at the table."

As she did not promptly answer the summons to dinner, Mme. De Réan sent her cousin Paul to find her.

"Sophie, Sophie," called Paul, at her room, "what are you doing? dinner is ready."

"Yes, yes, I am coming," she answered, walking backwards toward the dining-room, so that Paul might not see her clipped eye-brows.

She opened the door and entered the room. Scarcely had she set one foot within than every one looked at her and burst out laughing.

"What a face!" said M. De Réan.

She has cut her eye-brows!" replied Mme. De Réan.

"Oh! how funny, how funny she looks!" cried Paul. "What an astonishing change the mere cutting of the eye-brows makes in a face," said M. D' Aubert, Paul's father.

"I never saw such a singular looking face, remarked Mme. D' Aubert.

Meanwhile, Sophie stood with her arms hanging down at her side and head bent low, so confused she scarcely knew what to do or say. To add to it, her mother said in a moment or so, "Go to your room, miss; you are always in some mischief. Go, and do not make your appearance any more this evening."

Sophie obeyed, and the nurse was the next one to laugh when she beheld the fat red little face all shorn of its eye-brows. In vain did Sophie get very angry,—every one who saw her burst out laughing at first sight, and some advised her to pencil her brows with a piece of charcoal.

One day, Paul brought her a nice looking little package carefully tied with a string.

"Here, Sophie," said he, with a spice of mischief in his voice, "here is a present from my papa."

"What is it?" said Sophie, eagerly untying the string.

Opening the package, she beheld two very large, black, heavy eye-brows. "They are to be pasted on in place of those you cut off," he added. Sophie got very angry, and threw them at Paul, who laughing heartily ran from her.

Her eye-brows were more than six months in growing to their usual length; and even then they disappointed Sophie's expectations as to thickness, being very little, if any thicker than before. Sophie never again attempted to improve them.

IX.

The Horses' Bread.

SOPHIE was somewhat of a little glutton, always ready to eat. Her mother knowing that such indulgence is prejudicial to the health, had forbidden her to eat between meals; but Sophie paid no attention to this, and ate whenever she got a sly chance to do so.

Mme. De Réan was accustomed to go to the stables every day about two o'clock, to take bread and salt to M. De Réan's horses, more than a hundred in number.

Sophie always accompanied her mamma, and carried the basket filled with pieces of black bread, one piece of which she handed Mme. De Réan as they entered each stall. Her mother had positively forbidden her even to taste this bread, as being of inferior quality to that which she was accustomed to eating, and not thoroughly cooked, it might make her sick.

They finished up their rounds at the pony's stable. Sophie had a pony of her own, a present from her papa—a beautiful little animal, black and not larger than a small donkey ; and to him, she was always allowed to give the bread with her own hands. Often, she took a sly bite ere presenting it to him.

One day, when she felt more appetite than usual for this bread, she held the piece in her fingers in such a way as to leave but a tiny end for the pony.

" He will bite only as far as my fingers," said she, " and then I'll eat the rest."

So saying, she presented the bread to her pony, which immediately seized it, and also the end of her finger, biting her so violently that she dropped the bread. The pony now let go the finger to get his bread which he ate. Sophie could have shrieked from pain, but she dared not, lest this betray her to her mother.

Her finger bled so profusely that the blood ran down to the ground. Taking out her handkerchief, she bound it tightly around the bleeding finger; but as the handkerchief was soon soaking, she, at last, hid her hand under her apron, to prevent mamma's seeing the blood.

She gives bread to her Pony. (Page 76).

At dinner, however, she was obliged to use her hand which still bled a little; and in handling her spoon, glass, and bread, some drops of blood got on the table-cloth. Her mother perceived it.

"What is the matter with your hand, Sophie," said she, "there are spots of blood all around your plate."

Sophie made no reply.

MME. DE RÉAN.

Do you not hear what I say to you? what is the meaning of that blood on the table-cloth?

SOPHIE.

Mamma, ... it is ... it is ... from my finger.

MME. DE RÉAN.

What is the matter with your finger? When did you hurt it?

SOPHIE.

This morning, mamma, the pony bit me.

MME. DE RÉAN.

The pony that is as gentle as a lamb bit you! How did it happen?

SOPHIE.

I was giving him his bread, mamma.

MME. DE RÉAN.

Did you hold the bread in your open palm, as I have so often told you to do?

SOPHIE.

No, mamma, I held it between my fingers.

MME. DE RÉAN.

Well, then, since you have been so disobedient and foolish, you shall feed your pony no more.

Sophie took care not to reply, but she thought to herself that, in continuing to carry the basket of bread for the horses, which had not been forbidden her, she could easily slip a little of it for herself.

So, next morning, going with her mother to the stables, whilst the latter was giving the bread to the horses, Sophie slyly took a piece which she put in her pocket, to eat by degrees when her mother was not looking.

On reaching the stall of the last horse, the basket was empty; to Mme. De Réan's surprise, there was not a morsel for him. The groom assured her that he had put in the basket as many pieces of bread as there were horses but she showed him the empty basket. Whilst talking to him, however, she chanced to look towards Sophie, who, with distended jaws, was making a great effort to swallow the last mouthful of the bread she had taken. In vain did she try to gulp it down without even chewing it. Mme. De Réan perceived that she was eating, and knew at once that it must be the missing piece of bread which she had in her mouth.

Meanwhile, the disappointed horse expressed his impatience by pawing the ground and neighing.

"Little glutton," said Sophie's mother to her; "whilst my back was turned, you stole the poor horse's bread; and you also disobeyed me, for you know well that I have frequently forbidden you to eat it. Go, now, to your room, where you will dine to-day on bread-soup and bread since you are so fond of the latter; and, moreover, you will come with me no longer to feed the horses."

Hanging her head, Sophie went slowly to the house, and into her room.

"Dear me," said the nurse, "what a long face!

are you punished again? what new mischief have you been at now?"

"I did nothing but eat some of the horse's bread," answered Sophie, weeping. " I am so fond of it! The basket was so full that I didn't think mamma would find me out. And now, for this, I'm to have only soup and dry bread for my dinner," she continued, with a fresh outburst of grief.

The nurse looked at her with a smile of pity. She spoiled Sophie. Believing that Mme. De Réan was often too severe on the child, she not unfrequently sought means of consoling Sophie, and of lessening the severity of her punishments. So, when the servant brought Sophie's soup, with the piece of bread and glass of water that were intended for her dinner, the nurse set this meagre repast very ill-humoredly upon the table; and, going to an armoire in the room, she brought out a big piece of cheese, and a jar of preserves.

"Now," said she to Sophie, "eat first this cheese with your bread, and then take some preserves."

Seeing Sophie hesitate, she added:

"Your mamma sent you dry bread, but she

did not forbid my putting something on it for you."

SOPHIE.

But when mamma asks me, whether I had anything else given me, I must tell her, and then—

NURSE.

Tell her that I gave you some cheese and preserves, and insisted upon your eating them. I will explain to her that I did so, because mere dry bread is not good for the stomach.

Even prisoners are given something with their bread.

The nurse did very wrong in thus urging Sophie to eat slyly what her mamma had forbidden her; but Sophie was too young a child to see this; hence, she yielded without much persuasion, and dined heartily off of the cheese of which she was very fond, and the preserves of which she was still fonder. The nurse added a little wine to the glass of water, and, in place of desert, gave her some sweetened wine and water, in which Sophie soaked the remainder of her bread, thus making an excellent dinner.

"Now, do you know what you must do another time when punished, or when you want something to eat?" said nurse. "You must come to me, and I will find you something nice, something much better than that nasty black bread that horses and dogs eat."

Sophie promised her nurse that she would not forget, but would come to her every time she felt like having something nice to eat.

X.

THE CREAM AND WARM BREAD.

SOPHIE was a little glutton, as we have already stated; hence, she treasured up carefully what the nurse had said to her when giving her the cheese and preserves, and soon acted upon it.

One day, when she had eaten very little breakfast, because she knew the farmer's wife was to bring the nurse something good, she went to the latter and complained of hunger.

"How fortunate it is," said nurse, "that the farm-woman has just made me a present of some fresh brown bread, and a big jar of cream. Come, let me give you some of it, and you will see how nice it is."

Saying this, she placed upon the table the brown bread, all warm, and a large jar of thick, rich cream, which Sophie began to eat as if she were famished. Just as she had told

Sophie not to eat too much, it might make her sick. Mme. De Réan's voice was heard calling, "Lucie! Lucie!" (This was the nurse's name).

Lucie ran immediately to know her mistress's wishes. Madame De Réan told her that she desired some work to be prepared for Sophie. "She is now four years old, and it is time for her to be taught something useful," said Mme. De Réan.

NURSE.

But, Madame, what work could such a young child do?

MME. DE RÉAN.

"Prepare a napkin or a handkerchief for her to hem." Lucie made no reply, but retired in rather an ill humor.

Returning to her room, she found Sophie still eating. The jar of cream was almost empty, and an enormous piece of bread had disappeared.

"O gracious!" she exclaimed, as she was preparing Sophie's hemming, "you are going to make yourself sick! Is it possible that you

The cream jar was nearly empty. (Page 86).

have gulped down all that! What will your mamma say to me, if it makes you sick? You are going to get me a scolding."

SOPHIE.

Oh! don't be worried, nurse; I was very hungry, and what I have eaten will not make me sick. This cream and warm bread are delicious!"

NURSE.

Yes, but very heavy on the stomach. Gracious! what a quantity of bread you have eaten! I am almost sure you will be sick from this.

"Oh! no, no, my dear Lucie," answered Sophie embracing her, "don't be the least uneasy; I assure you, I feel very well."

Lucie now gave her the little handkerchief to be hemmed, telling her to take it to her mamma, who would impart to her the necessary instructions.

Sophie ran immediately to the room where Mme. De Réan was, and presented the handkerchief. Mme. De Réan took much pains in teaching her how to put the needle in and draw it out. The beginning of Sophie's hem was very badly done, but after a little while of continued effort, there was great improvement and Sophie rather liked her new employment.

"Mamma," said she, "will you please let me go show my work to nurse?"

"Yes," answered her mother, "then come back, and put it up, and play in my room."

Sophie carrying the handkerchief, ran to the nurse who was really astonished to see it nearly hemmed and so well. She inquired a little anxiously of Sophie how her stomach felt, whether she had any pain in it.

"No, no, nurse," answered Sophie, "but I am no longer hungry."

"I certainly believe that," said the nurse, "after all you have eaten. "But hurry back to your mother, for fear she scolds you."

Sophie returned to the sitting room, put her work up, and getting out her toys, was soon absorbed in play. Whilst playing, she began to feel ill at ease—the cream and bread had commenced to turn on her stomach, and her head ached. Sitting down in her little chair, she remained motionless and with eyes closed.

Noticing the stillness, Mme. De Réan turned

to see what was the matter, and perceived Sophie as we have just described her, pale and apparently suffering.

"Are you sick, Sophie?" she inquired anxiously.

"Yes, mamma, my head aches."

"How long has it been aching?"

"Since I finished putting up my work."

"Have you been eating since breakfast?"

Sophie hesitated a moment, and then said in a very low tone,

"No, mamma, nothing at all."

"I perceive that you are not speaking the truth; so, I will ask your nurse, who will tell me.

Madame De Réan left the room, and returned in a few minutes, apparently very angry.

"You have lied to me, Miss; for your nurse acknowledges that she gave you some cream and warm bread of which you ate ravenously. So much the worse for you; for you are going to be sick, which will prevent your dining to-morrow at your aunt D'Aubert's with your cousin Paul, Camille and Madeleine De Fleurville. Instead of playing with them, and hunting strawberries in the woods, you will have to stay at home, and eat nothing but soup."

Taking hold of Sophie's hand, which she found very hot, Mme. De Réan led her towards the bed.

"Give Sophie nothing whatever to eat until to-morrow;" said she to the nurse; "meanwhile, make her drink a little barley water, or orange-leaf water; and I tell you now, that if you ever repeat this morning's offence, I will send you away immediately."

The nurse feeling guilty, made no reply; and Sophie, now quite sick, let herself be put to bed without saying a word. She spent a miserable night, restless, sick at her stomach, and her head aching violently. Towards morning, she slept; and on awaking, although her head still ached a little, she felt greatly revived by the fresh morning air. She passed a sad day indeed, regretting that she had not been able to dine with her aunt. For two days longer, she was still very poorly. From that time forth, Sophie never again could eat cream or warm bread—she had taken such a disgust for them.

She sometimes went with her cousin and other friends to the farm-houses in the vicinity and whilst all around her partook of the delicious cream and brown bread set out before them, Sophie could not even taste of the repast, the very sight of the thick, frothy cream and farm bread recalling her sufferings so vividly, as almost to turn her stomach. After this little spell of sickness, she also paid much more attention to mamma's words than to those of the nurse. The latter did not retain her position much longer. Mme. De Réan having lost confidence in her, dismissed her, and supplied her place by a reliable person who never allowed Sophie to do what her mamma had forbidden her.

XI.

The Squirrel.

ONE day, Sophie and Paul were taking a walk in a little piece of woods composed of oaks, and very near the château. They were both gathering acorns, out of which they made baskets, shoes and boats. Suddenly an acorn fell on Sophie's back; and whilst stooping to pick it up, she felt another strike the edge of her ear.

"Paul! Paul!" said she, "come see these acorns that have just fallen upon me; look, they are all bitten. What could it be way up there gnawing them like this? Mice don't climb trees, and birds don't eat acorns."

Paul took the acorns in his hands, examined them, and then raising his head, he exclaimed:

"It's a squirrel! I see him! he is on a very high branch, and looking down at us in defiance."

Sophie followed Paul's glance, and saw a pretty little squirrel, with a superb tail standing out like a plume. He was wiping his face with his fore-paws. From time to time, he would look at Sophie and Paul, and then spring upon another branch.

"Oh! how I should love to have that squirrel!" said Sophie. "What a pretty little fellow he is! and how nice it would be for me to have him to play with, to take out walking, and to attend to."

PAUL.

It would be easy enough to trap him; but, Sophie, squirrels make a room smell bad, and they gnaw everything.

SOPHIE.

Oh! I wouldn't leave my things where he could gnaw them. I would lock them up out of his way. And I would clean his cage twice a day. But how could we get him.

PAUL.

I should get a cage rather large, and put in it walnuts, hazel nuts, almonds—whatever squirrels are fond of. Then, leaving the door open, (a string, however, tied to the door), I should set the cage under the oak, and hide somewhere very near. I should watch all the while, and when he was fairly in the cage, eating the delicacies prepared for him, I should suddenly pull the string, the door would close, and Mr. Squirrel be caught.

SOPHIE.

But perhaps he wouldn't go into the cage; he might be afraid.

PAUL.

Oh! there's not the least danger of his not going in the cage; squirrels are gluttons, and he can't resist the walnuts and almonds.

SOPHIE.

Trap him, then, I beg you, dear Paul; it would give me so much pleasure to have him.

PAUL.

But your mamma—would she be willing?

SOPHIE.

Oh, yes! let us both beg her so earnestly that she will give her consent.

The two children ran immediately to the

house. Paul was charged with the responsibility of presenting the case to Mme. De Réan, who, at first, refused to grant their request, but finally yielded, saying, however, to Sophie:

"I warn you that this squirrel will soon annoy you enough: he will climb everywhere; he will gnaw your books, your playthings—anything he can get hold of; he will smell bad—in a word, he will be unbearable."

SOPHIE.

Oh! no, mamma; I promise you to keep such a watch over him, that he'll do no mischief whatever.

MME. DE RÉAN.

First of all, remember, that he is never to come near my room, nor the parlor; you are to keep him in your own room all the time.

SOPHIE.

Yes, mamma, he shall always stay in my room, except when I take him out for an airing.

Delighted with the granted permission, Sophie and Paul hastened to hunt up a cage. In the lumber-room they found one which had formerly been used for a squirrel. Bringing it forth, with the nurse's aid they dusted it and brushed it clean, and then put in it some walnuts, hazel nuts, and fresh almonds.

SOPHIE.

Come quick, and set the cage under the oak. I hope the squirrel is still there.

PAUL.

Wait until I tie this string to the door. The string must be passed through the bars, so that when I give it a pull the door shuts immediately.

SOPHIE.

I am afraid the squirrel will be gone.

PAUL.

Oh! no, he will stay just where he is, or some place very near until night. There, now, it is ready; pull the string to try it.

Sophie pulled the string, and the door closed instantly. The children delighted, took the cage to the little woods. Approaching the oak in which they had seen the squirrel, they sought in vain for a glimpse of him; nor were the branches or leaves stirring. Disappointed, they were just about to move on and continue their search under some of the other oaks, when there glanced against Sophie's forehead an acorn, bitten just like those that had fallen on her in the morning.

"He is here! he is here!" she exclaimed. "There! I see him! I see the end of his tail from behind that thick branch."

And indeed the squirrel, hearing their voices, poked out his little head to see what was going on.

"That's right, my dear," said Paul. "There you are; you will soon be in prison. Come, see the nice things we've brought you to eat; be a little glutton, pet, be a little glutton; and you will find out how gluttony is punished."

The poor squirrel, utterly unconscious of the designs upon his liberty, of which he was so soon to be deprived, looked at him with a most mischievous air, turning his head first to one side and then to the other. Seeing Paul place the cage on the ground, he cast an envious eye upon the walnuts and almonds within. When the children had concealed themselves behind the trunk of the oak, he cautiously descended two or three branches, stopped, looked all around, then came down a little farther, until, by degrees, he was at the cage. He first ran one paw and then the other between the bars; but, not being able to reach the nuts, and the almonds looking more and more appetizing, he sought a means of entering the cage. It was not long before he found the door. Here he hesitated, looked at the string with a mistrustful air, and then stretched out a paw to its utmost, hoping still to get at the nuts thus. Not succeeding, he risked entering the cage. Scarcely was he fairly in, than the children, who, with palpitating hearts, had been watching his every movement, pulled the string, and the squirrel was a prisoner. Filled with fright, he dropped the almond he had begun to gnaw, and eagerly sought a means of escape from the cage. But, alas! the poor little creature had to pay the price of his gluttony, and remain a prisoner. The children darted towards the cage. Paul, taking care to see that the door was securely fastened, picked up their prize, and carried it to Sophie's room. Sophie, having ran on ahead, and in a tone of great triumph, called her nurse to come, see the new pet.

The nurse did not seem pleased to see it.

"What are you going to do with this animal?" said she. "It will bite us, and the noise it will make gnawing and nibbling all the time, will be unbearable. What was your idea, Sophie, in taking upon yourself the care of this ugly thing?"

SOPHIE.

Let me tell you, nurse, first, that it is not ugly at all; the squirrel is a very pretty creature; and, again, that my squirrel is not going to make any noise, nor is it going to bite any one. I intend to take sole charge of it.

NURSE.

Indeed? Well, then, I pity the poor animal. It will soon be left to starve.

SOPHIE, (*indignantly*).

Starve! certainly not. I shall feed it on hazel nuts, almonds, bread, sugar, wine.

NURSE, (*in a tone of derision*).

What a well-fed squirrel! sugar will spoil his teeth, and wine make him tipsy.

The squirrel came down, halted, looking on all sides. (Page 100).

PAUL.

Ha! ha! ha! a tipsy squirrel! how funny that would be!

SOPHIE.

It will not be funny at all, Sir; for my squirrel is not going to get tipsy, He is going to behave sensibly.

NURSE.

We shall see. The first thing we must do is to get him some straw for a bed. He seems frightened. I don't believe he will let you handle him. He is not at all pleased at his being captured.

SOPHIE.

I am going to pet him a little, to get him accustomed to me, and make him understand that no one will harm him.

With this, Sophie put her hand in the cage; the affrighted squirrel drew back into a corner. Sophie reached out a little farther to take hold of him, but just as she was about to pick him up, he bit her finger. With a loud shriek of pain, she drew forth her hand, from which the blood was trickling. The cage door being open, the squirrel darted out, and began to run around the room, the nurse and Paul pursuing him. He was almost captured, when suddenly making a spring, he eluded them, and commenced running around the room again. Sophie, forgetting her bleeding finger, joined her nurse and Paul in the chase. This continued for about half an hour, and the poor squirrel was now so tired out, that he must inevitably have been taken in a few minutes, had he not espied an open window. With one bound, he was beyond his pursuers, and, climbing up the wall outside the window, he reached the roof of the house.

Sophie, Paul, and the nurse, all ran down to the garden. Looking up, they beheld their pet seated on the roof, and half dead from fatigue and fear.

Oh! what must we do, nurse? what must we do?" exclaimed Sophie.

"Leave him there," answered nurse. "He has bitten you already; just leave him there."

SOPHIE.

But he doesn't know me yet; he would not

have bitten me if he had known me. When he finds out that I feed him, he will love me.

PAUL.
I don't believe he can ever be taught to love

you: he is too old to be tamed. We must get a very young one, if we wish to tame it.

SOPHIE.

Oh, Paul! do throw a ball at him to make him come down. We can catch him if he does, and shut him up again.

PAUL.

I will throw at him, but really I don't believe he'll come down.

Saying this, Paul got a big foot-ball which he launched at the squirrel, and, unfortunately, his aim was more skillful than he meant it to be—for the persecuted little creature was struck in the head. Both ball and squirrel descended to the ground; the former bounded and rebounded, but the latter, with head all bleeding, his sides and paws broken and crushed by the fall, did not stir. Sophie and Paul ran to pick him up, and found, to their grief and astonishment, that he was dead.

"You wicked Paul!" said Sophie, "you have killed my squirrel!"

PAUL.

It is all your fault, for you told me to throw

at him with a ball, and make him come down.

SOPHIE.

I wanted you only to frighten him, not to kill him.

PAUL.

And I did not intend to kill him; I didn't know I was so expert; the ball took him by surprise.

SOPHIE.

You are not expert, Sir; you are downright cruel and bad. Go away from me, I don't love you any more.

PAUL.

And as for me, I detest you. You are sillier than the squirrel. I am delighted that I have saved him from being tormented by you.

SOPHIE.

You are a bad boy, sir; I'll never play with you again, and I'll never ask you to do anything for me any more.

PAUL.

So much the better, Miss; I shall only be

that much more at my ease, and not forever puzzling my brain to help on your tom-foolery.

NURSE.

See here, children, instead of disputing, why don't you acknowledge that you acted without reflection, and that you are both guilty of the squirrel's death. Poor little creature! he is better off now than when alive; at least, he suffers no longer. I am going to call some one to take him up and put him out of sight. Do you, Sophie, go to your room and bathe your finger in water. I will soon rejoin you there.

Sophie went to her room, followed by Paul, who, being really a good child, without the least trace of resentment in his disposition, forgave all that she had just said to him, and instead of pouting, kindly helped her to pour some water in a basin, and bathe her hand in it. When the nurse came, she wrapped Sophie's finger up in lettuce-leaf, and tied a rag around it. The children were a little ashamed when they went to dinner, to have to recount so sad an ending of their adventure with the squirrel.

Their fathers and mothers made fun of them.

The cage was taken back to the lumber-room. Sophie's finger kept sore for several days, after which time, she thought no more about the squirrel, except to say that she would never have another.

XII.

THE TEA.

IT was the 19th of July, the anniversary of Sophie's birth. She was four years old.

Her mamma always made her a pretty birthday present, but she never told her in advance what it was. Sophie, to-day, arose much earlier than usual, and urged the nurse to dress her as fast as possible, so that she might hasten to mamma and get her birthday present.

"Quick, quick, nurse, I beg you," said she; "I am so anxious to know what mamma is going to give me."

NURSE.

But do let me have time to comb your hair. You certainly wouldn't wish to go to your mamma in such a trim, your hair in disorder like it is now. That wouldn't be a beautiful way of beginning your fourth birthday. Keep still, you wriggle about so.

SOPHIE.

Oh! oh! you pull my hair so, nurse.

NURSE.

That's because you keep moving your head. There it is again! How can I guess what side it pleases you to turn your head to.

At last, dressed and her hair combed, Sophie ran joyously to her mamma.

"How early you are, Sophie, this morning," said Mme. De Réan, smiling. "I see that you have not forgotten your fourth birthday, and the present I owe you. Here is a book for you; I think you will find it very entertaining."

Sophie thanked her mamma in an embarrassed manner, and took the book which was bound in red morocco.

"What can I do with this book?" thought she. "Of what use will it be to me? I can't read."

Her mother looked at her, and smiling, said:

"You don't seem pleased with my present, and yet it is very pretty. It is marked on the outside, *Art*. I am sure you will find it more entertaining than you imagine.

SOPHIE.

I don't know, mamma.

MME. DE RÉAN.

Open it, and you will see.

Sophie attempted to open the book, but, to her surprise, she could not; and, moreover, on turning it, she heard a noise as if something within it moved. In astonishment, she looked at her mother, who now laughed heartily, and said to her:

"This is an extraordinary book,—not at all like other books which open of themselves,—to open this, you must press your thumb upon the edge of it, just about the middle of the book."

With this, she pressed it gently; it opened, and Sophie beheld with delight, not a book, but a beautiful box of colors, with brushes, tiny saucers for rubbing the paints on ere using, and twelve little sketch-books full of charming pictures to be painted.

"Oh! thanks, dear mamma!" exclaimed Sophie. "How happy I am! It is lovely."

MME. DE RÉAN.

You were a little surprised and disappointed a moment ago, when you thought I had given you a book; but I would not have played such a joke on you. You can amuse yourself painting to-day, with your cousin, Paul, and your friends, Camille and Madeleine, whom I have invited to spend the day with you. They will be here at two o'clock. Your aunt, D'Aubert, has charged me with presenting you this little tea-set. She cannot come herself until three o'clock, and she wished you to receive her present in the morning.

The delighted child took the waiter with its six little cups, a tea-pot, sugar-bowl, and cream-jug. She asked her mother's permission to make some real tea for her friends.

"No," replied Mme. De Réan, "you will spill the cream everywhere, and burn yourself with the tea. Play having tea, and that will be just as nice."

Sophie said nothing, but she was not pleased at the refusal.

"What's the use of having a tea-set," said she to herself, "if I am not allowed to put anything in it? My playmates will laugh at me. I must really hunt up something to fill it. Perhaps the nurse can help me.

Saying to her mother that she was going now to show the nurse her presents, Sophie picked up her paint-box and tea-set, and hastened to her room.

SOPHIE.

Look, nurse, look at the pretty things mamma and aunt D'Aubert, have given me.

NURSE.

Oh, the lovely tea-set! How you can amuse yourself with that! But I don't like the book. What use is a book to you, who can't read?

SOPHIE, (*laughing*).

Bravo! Nurse is caught just as I was. It is not a book, nurse, it's a paint-box.

And Sophie opened the box, which the nurse declared lovely. After talking about how she would spend the day, Sophie told the nurse that she (Sophie) had desired to make her playmates some real tea, but mamma had refused to let her do so.

"What can I put in my little tea-pot, my sugar-bowl, and my cream-jug?" she continued. "Couldn't you help me, dear nurse, to get something for my friends to eat or drink?"

"No, little one," answered the nurse, "I really could not. Don't you remember that your mamma told me she would dismiss me, if ever I gave you anything to eat when she had forbidden it?"

Sophie sighed, and seemed lost in thought. Gradually, however, her face brightened—an idea had struck her. We shall soon learn what the idea was, and whether good or not. Sophie played for some time, then breakfasted. Returning from a walk with her mother, she said she must now put everything in readiness for the arrival of her friends. The paint-box was set out upon a table, and, upon an another table, were displayed the six cups, arranged in a circle around the sugar-bowl, tea-pot, and cream-jug.

"Now," said Sophie, "I shall make some tea."

Going out in the garden, and gathering a few clover-leaves, she put them in the tea-pot. Next, she went to the dog's house, and picking up the vessel of water placed there for her mamma's dog to drink, she poured some of this on the clover-leaves.

"There!" said she, delighted, "there's the tea! Now, I am going to make the cream."

Taking a piece of whitening, used for cleaning silver, she scraped a little of it into the cream-jug, poured some of the dog's drinking water on it, and stirred it well with a spoon. When the mixture looked very white, she set it on the table. Nothing remained now for her to prepare but the sugar. Breaking off little

pieces of this same whitening with her knife, she dropped them in the sugar-bowl, which, when filled, she placed on the table, and then stood, regarding the whole with an air of admiration.

"There," said she, rubbing her hands in delight, "it is splendid! I do believe I'm real smart! I bet neither Paul nor any of the rest of my playmates would ever have thought of such a thing!"

Sophie was obliged to await the arrival of her friends a full half hour after this, but she did not grow weary. So pleased was she with her latest device, the tea, that she could not keep away from the little table, on which the tea-set was displayed, but continued to walk around it, looking at it admiringly, rubbing her hands, and repeating:

"Oh! but I am smart! I am smart!"

At last, Paul and the others arrived. Sophie ran to meet them, embraced them affectionately, and then hastened to take them into the room where the presents were. They were all, at first, deceived by the paint-box, just as Sophie herself and the nurse had been. The tea-set, they declared lovely, and were eager to use it immediately; but Sophie begged them to wait until three o'clock. They then amused themselves with the paints, each one taking a little sketch-book. After some time, when they had had enough of this, and everything was put to rights, Paul said:

"Now, let's have the tea."

"Yes, yes," echoed the little girls in unison.

CAMILLE.

You do the honors of the table, Sophie.

SOPHIE.

Yes; come, all seat yourselves.... There now, that's it.... Hand me your cups to put the sugar in them.... Now, the tea, and lastly, the cream. Drink now.

MADELEINE.

It is very strange that this sugar doesn't melt.

SOPHIE.

Stir it well and it will melt.

PAUL.

But the tea is cold.

SOPHIE.

No wonder! it has been made so long.

CAMILLE, (*tasting the tea, and spitting it out in disgust*).

Ugh! What horrid stuff is this? It is not tea at all.

MADELEINE, (*spitting out hers also*).

This is detestable! It smells like chalk.

PAUL, (*following Camille's and Madeleine's example*).

Oh, Sophie! what have you given us? It is nasty, disgusting!

SOPHIE, (*greatly embarrassed*).

Find out!

PAUL.

What did you say? find out? It is a shame for you to play such a trick on us! You deserve to have us make you drink your detestable tea.

SOPHIE, (*getting angry*).

You are all so hard to please, that nothing seems good to you.

CAMILLE, (*smiling*).

You must acknowledge, Sophie, that a person not hard to please, couldn't help finding this tea miserable stuff.

PAUL, (*holding the tea-pot up to Sophie*).

Take a drink yourself, and then you'll find out whether we are hard to please or not.

SOPHIE, (*resisting him*).

Let me alone, Paul; you worry me.

PAUL, (*continuing*).

Ah! we are hard to please and you find the tea good! Drink some of it then and your cream too.

Saying this, Paul seized Sophie and poured

her tea, such detestable, disgusting stuff that the mere tasting it made one sick at the stomach; and when we complained, she said we were all too hard to please.

Mme. De Réan picked up the cream jug, smelt it, and then tasted it with the end of her tongue. With a gesture of disgust she said to Sophie.

"Where, Miss, did you get this horrid make-believe cream."

SOPHIE, (*with head hung and greatly confused.*)

I made it, mamma.

MME. DE RÉAN.

You made it! with what? answer me.

SOPHIE, (*abashed as already mentioned.*)

With the whitening for cleaning silver and the dog's drinking water.

MME. DE RÉAN.

And this tea, what is it made of?

SOPHIE, (*abashed as already mentioned.*)

Clover leaves and the dog's drinking water.

Mme. de Réan, (*examining the sugar bowl.*)

Stale water and chalk! You have regaled your friends truly admirably; and you have begun your fourth birthday well, miss, disobeying me when I forbade your having tea, attempting to make your friends drink this disgusting so-called tea, and fighting with your cousin. I now take possession of the tea-set to prevent a repetition of such a scene, and I should send you to dine in your room, were I not unwilling to spoil the pleasure of your little friends who are so good, and who would suffer, I know, at your being punished.

The mothers retired, laughing in spite of themselves at Sophie's ridiculous entertainment. The children remained alone. Paul and Sophie were so ashamed of their conduct that they dared not look at each other. Camille and Madeleine, embraced, consoled and endeavored to reconcile them. Sophie embraced Paul, asked pardon of all and everything was forgotten. They now ran out to play in the garden, where they caught eight superb butterflies, which Paul put in a box having a glass cover.

The remainder of the afternoon they spent in arranging the box that the butterflies might be well lodged,—putting in it grass, flowers, some drops of sugared water, strawberries and cherries.

When evening came, and each had to leave, Paul took the box home with him, at the urgent entreaties of Sophie, Camille, and Madeleine, who all saw how anxious he was to have it.

XIII

The Wolves.

SOPHIE was very disobedient as our readers no doubt have perceived from that portion of her history already related. This fault of disobedience should have been corrected, but it had not yet been; consequently, she was always in trouble.

The day after her fourth birthday, her mother called her and said to her.

"Sophie, I promised you that when you were four years old, I would let you accompany me on some of my long afternoon walks. To-day, I am going to the Svitine farm and by way of the woods. You may come with me, but you must be careful not to lag behind; you know I walk very rapidly, and if you stop along the road, you might be left far behind me without my perceiving it.

Sophie delighted, promised her mamma to keep very close to her, so as not to get lost in the woods.

To Sophie's great joy, Paul arrived, just as she and her mamma were about to start, and he asked to be allowed to accompany them.

For some time, they walked steadily along, close behind Mme. De Réan, amusing themselves watching the big dogs that she always took with, run and jump and frisk around her.

Reaching the woods, the children picked some flowers which were in their way, but without stopping.

Sophie now perceived very near the road, a number of strawberry vines, loaded with strawberries.

"Oh!" she exclaimed, "such beautiful strawberries! What a pity, for them to be left there, not eaten!"

Hearing the exclamation, Mme. De Réan looked back, and again forbade Sophie's stopping.

The latter sighed and cast a longing eye upon the strawberries.

"Don't look at them," said Paul, "and then you'll not think about them any more."

SOPHIE.

Oh! but they are so red, so beautiful, so ripe! They must be delicious!

PAUL.

The more you look at them, the more you'll want them. And since aunt forbids your stopping to pick them, what good can it do you to keep looking at them?

SOPHIE.

I want to get just one, and that will not delay us much. Stay with me, and we will eat it together.

PAUL.

No, I don't wish to disobey aunt, nor do I wish to get lost in the woods.

SOPHIE.

But there is no danger of our getting lost. Mamma said that to make us afraid. We could easily catch up to her, if we did stay behind a little.

PAUL.

No; I am going to obey aunt. This is a very dense woods, and we couldn't find our way if we once got separated from her any distance.

SOPHIE.

Do as you please, then, coward; as for me, the very next place I come to and see such strawberries as those we have just passed, I am going to help myself.

PAUL.

I am not a coward, Miss; and you,—you are very disobedient, and a glutton; so, get lost in the woods, if you choose; I prefer obeying aunt.

Paul continued to follow Mme. De Réan, who surrounded by her dogs, walked rapidly and without looking back. Soon, Sophie perceived a place where the strawberries appeared as tempting as those she had seen at first. Tasting one, she found it delicious; she tried a second and a third. She then changed her position to one in which she could pick the berries more at her ease and faster, from time to time, casting a glance towards her mamma and Paul, now at a considerable distance from her. The dogs all at once, began to act strangely, showing great signs of uneasiness, going towards the woods and then returning to Mme. De Réan. At last, they pressed so close around her that she looked to see what had frightened them; and, to her horror, she caught the gleam of wild, ferocious eyes, amid the undergrowth of the dense woods, hearing, at the same time, a noise of broken twigs and the rustling of dry leaves. Turning to tell the children to walk ahead of her, what was her fright to see only Paul!

"Where is Sophie?" she exclaimed.

PAUL.

She stayed behind, aunt, to eat strawberries.

MME. DE RÉAN.

Oh! unhappy child, what has she done! We are followed by wolves! Let us hasten back to save her, if there is yet time.

Mme. De Réan, with poor terrified Paul and the dogs ran at full speed towards the spot where they supposed Sophie to be. They perceived her from a distance, seated amid the strawberries which she was quietly eating. Suddenly, two of the dogs, uttering a plaintive cry, almost flew towards her. At the same moment, the head of an enormous wolf with gleaming eyes and open mouth was seen peering from amid the woods close by. Seeing the dogs, he hesitated an instant; but the next, he rushed toward her, believing that he could have time before they reached him, to carry her off to the woods, where he might afterwards devour her. The dogs beholding their little mistress's danger, and urged on by the terrified cries of Mme. De Réan and Paul, redoubled their speed, and came upon the wolf, just as he had caught Sophie by the skirts to drag her into the woods. Attacked by the dogs, he relinquished his hold on Sophie, to battle with them. The arrival upon the scene of two other wolves that had also followed Mme. De Réan, and now come to the rescue of their companion, made the situation of the poor dogs perilous in the extreme; but the faithful creatures fought so valiantly that the wolves were soon put to flight. The dogs covered with blood and wounds, now licked Mme. De Réan's hands, and those of the children who during the combat, had stood trembling in every limb. Mme. De Réan returned their caresses, and began to retrace her steps towards home, hold-

The wolf feeling himself bitten by the dogs released Sophie. (Page 136).

ing each child by the hand, and surrounded by her intrepid defenders.

She made Sophie no reproaches—poor Sophie, who trembling with fright could scarcely walk. Nor was Paul less pale and frightened. At last, emerging from the woods, they were near a little stream.

"Let us stop here," said Mme. De Réan," and all take a drink of this fresh water; it will revive us a little after our fright."

Bending over the stream, she drank a few drops, and then bathed her face and hands. The children followed her example. She told them to wet their heads also with the cool water; which they did, and found themselves, in consequence, recovering their composure and greatly refreshed.

The poor dogs all plunged into the stream, drinking of it, rolling over in it and laving their wounds therein. Emerging from their bath, they too were cleansed and greatly revived.

After resting about a quarter of an hour, Mme. De Réan arose to depart. The children kept very close to her.

"Sophie," said she, "don't you believe now

that I was right in forbidding you to stop along the way?"

SOPHIE.

Oh! yes, yes, mamma, and I beg your pardon for having disobeyed you. And yours too, my good Paul; I am very sorry for having called you a coward.

MME. DE RÉAN.

Coward! you called him a coward! Do you know that when we ran to you, it was he who went ahead? Do you also know that when the other wolves came to their comrades assistance Paul, armed only with a stick which he picked up as he ran, tried to intercept their way, and moreover that I had to catch him up in my arms, and forcibly restrain him from helping the dogs? Did you also notice that during the whole of the combat, Paul kept always in the foreground, to prevent the wolves reaching us? This is the kind of a coward Paul is!

Sophie threw herself on Paul's neck; embracing him affectionately, and saying, "Thanks, thanks, my good Paul, my dear Paul, I shall always love you with my whole heart."

When they reached home, every one was astonished at their pale faces and Sophie's torn skirts.

Mme. De Réan recounted their adventure; and all who heard it praised Paul's obedience

and courage, censured Sophie for her disobedience and gluttony and admired the valor of the dogs, which were loaded with caresses, and

given an excellent dinner of bones and scraps of meat.

Next day, Mme. De Réan presented Paul a complete Zouave uniform. Almost wild with joy, he immediately put it on, and hastened to find Sophie. She shrieked with fright at seeing this Turk come into her room, a turban on his head, sabre in hand and pistols at his belt. But Paul bursting into a laugh and commencing to play, she recognized him, and declared him charming in his uniform.

Sophie's mamma did not punish her for her disobedience in the woods, believing that her little daughter's fright had been sufficient punishment, and that the offence would never be repeated.

XIV.

THE SCRATCHED CHEEK.

SOPHIE was very quick tempered—another fault of which we have not yet spoken.

One day, she was amusing herself painting in one of her little sketch books, and Paul was cutting cards to make salad baskets, tables and benches out of them. They were seated at the same little table, facing each other. In moving his legs, Paul shook the table.

"Take care, do," said Sophie, in an impatient tone; "you shake the table, I can't paint."

For a few moments, Paul was very careful; then, he forgot and accidentally shook the table again.

"Paul, you are unbearable! "exclaimed Sophie, " I have already told you once that you hinder me from painting."

PAUL.

Ah! bah! as to the pretty things you paint, it is not worth inconveniencing one's self for them.

SOPHIE.

I know very well that you don't inconvenience yourself, but as you do inconvenience me, I beg you to keep your legs still.

PAUL, (*laughing at her*).

My legs wont keep still; they move in spite of me.

SOPHIE, (*getting angry*).

I'll tie a string to them—these annoying legs, and then, if they still move, I'll chase them away.

PAUL.

Just try a little of that; and you'll find out what the feet at the end of these legs can do.

SOPHIE.

You wicked boy, would you kick me?

PAUL.

Certainly, if you attempted to use your fists on me.

At this, Sophie worked up into a passion, threw some water in Paul's face, and he getting angry in turn, gave the table a kick which upset it and all that was on it. Sophie darted at Paul and scratched his face so hard that the blood trickled down his cheeks. Paul cried out, but Sophie, now completely carried away by temper, continued to slap and pummel him, until Paul who really did not wish to fight her, at last, took refuge in a little room adjoining and locked the door. Vainly did Sophie rap, Paul paid no attention to her whatever. In a short time Sophie's anger was over; she grew calm, and now began to repent of what she had done, especially when she remembered that Paul had risked his life to save her from the wolves.

"O my poor Paul!" thought she, how dreadfully I have treated him. "What can I do to put him in a good humor. I shouldn't like to beg his pardon; but it is so trying to have to say, 'Pardon me.' "Yet," she added, after a little reflection, "it is a great deal more shameful to behave as I have just been behaving, and how can Paul pardon me, if I don t ask him to do so?"

Having pondered the matter thus a few moments, Sophie arose and rapped gently at the locked door between Paul and herself. "Paul, Paul," she called in a quiet, humble tone; but there was no reply. "Paul," she continued in the same gentle manner, "my dear Paul, please pardon me, I am very, very sorry I was so bad, and treated you so shamefully. Indeed, I will never do it any more."

The door was quietly opened a little way, and Paul's head appeared. He looked at Sophie with mistrust.

"Have you gotten over your anger? really?" said he.

"Oh! yes, yes, indeed, I have, dear Paul; and I am very sorry for having been so bad."

Paul opened the door wide, and Sophie raising her eyes, beheld with grief how she had scratched his face. With a cry, she fell upon Paul's neck.

"Oh! my poor Paul!" said she, "how I

have hurt you! how I have scratched you!
What can I do to heal your face?"

"That's nothing," replied Paul, "it will all
come off of itself. Let us get a basin and some
water. When the blood is washed off my face,
it will be all right again."

Sophie ran to help Paul get a basin full of
water; but vainly did he bathe his face, rub
and wipe it,—the scratches showed very plainly. Sophie was distressed beyond measure.

"What will mamma say?" she murmured,
"what will she say? She will be very angry
with me, and punish me severely, I know."

Paul, a most forgiving child was also distressed, and could think of nothing except
how to avert Sophie's anticipated punishment.

"I can't say I got scratched by thorns, because that would not be true," said he. "But,
oh! just wait now, and you'll see what I can
do."

Paul immediately starts off in a run, followed
by Sophie. He goes into the little woods near
the house and directing his steps towards a
holly-bush, he dashes into it, and turns himself about in such a manner as to be pricked
and scratched by the sharp, pointed leaves.

He comes out of it looking worse scratched than before.

When Sophie saw his face all bleeding, she could not restrain her tears.

"Oh!" said she, "I am the cause of your sufferings, my poor Paul! It is to prevent my being punished that you have scratched your-

self worse than I scratched you in my passion!
Oh! dear Paul, how good you are! How I
love you!"

"Let us go to the house," he replied, "as
fast as we can, so that I can bathe my face.
Oh! don't look so sad, my poor Sophie. Indeed, I suffer very little, and to-morrow, my
face will not hurt me at all. I ask you now
not to tell that you scratched me. If you do,
I shall be very sorry, and there will have been
no use in my rolling in the holly-bush. Do
you promise me?"

"Yes," said Sophie, embracing him, "I will
do all that you wish."

They went to Sophie's room and Paul bathed
his face. When they entered the parlor, their
mammas, both exclaimed at sight of his
scratched and swollen face:

"How did you do that, my poor Paul?"
asked Mme. D'Aubert. "One might suppose
you had been rolling among thorns."

PAUL.

That is just what has happened, mamma.
I ran into a holly-bush, and in struggling to
get out of it, my face and hands were well
scratched.

MME. D'AUBERT.

You were very awkward to have fallen into the holly; and you should not have struggled, but have extricated yourself gently.

MME. DE RÉAN.

Where then were you, Sophie? You should have helped Paul to arise.

PAUL.

She ran after me, aunt; but before she had time to assist me, I was already up.

Mme. D'Aubert led Paul out of the room to put some cucumber ointment on his scratches. Sophie remained with her mamma, who feeling somewhat suspicious of her little daughter, eyed her attentively.

MME. DE RÉAN.

Why are you sad; Sophie?

SOPHIE; (*blushing*).

I am not sad, mamma.

MME. DE RÉAN.

Oh! yes, indeed you are; you are as sad and anxious as if something tormented you.

SOPHIE, (*in a quivering voice, and with tears in her eyes*).

Nothing is the matter, mamma; nothing is the matter with me.

MME. DE RÉAN.

Yes, there is, for I see that even in telling me there is nothing the matter, you are ready to cry.

SOPHIE, (*sobbing aloud*).

I. . . . I. . . . can't . . . tell you. . . . I . . I . . promised Paul. . . . not. . . . to tell . . . you.

MME. DE RÉAN, (*trying to soothe and encourage Sophie*).

Listen to me, Sophie; if Paul has done something wrong, you should not keep your promise to him of not telling me. I now promise you that I will not scold him for it nor will I tell his mamma. I wish to know what makes you so sad, and why you cry so bitterly, and you must tell me.

Sophie buried her face in her mother's lap and was not able to speak for sobs.

The latter continued to sooth and encourage her, and, at last Sophie said.

"Paul has done nothing wrong, mamma; on the contrary he has been very good, and done a noble thing. It is I who was bad, and poor Paul to keep me from being scolded and punished rolled in the holly-bush.

More surprised then ever at this, Mme. De Réan questioned Sophie, who now recounted all that had passed between Paul and herself.

"Noble little Paul!" exclaimed Mme. De Réan; "what a good heart he has! What courage and kindness! And you, my dear Sophie,—what a difference there is between you and your cousin! Just see how you have let your temper carry you away in being guilty of such behavior to this excellent Paul, who always forgives and forgets your acts of injustice, and who, to-day again has been so generous to you. He should not however, have told a fib to screen you, as truthfulness is a very great virtue.

SOPHIE.

Oh! yes, mamma, I see indeed how bad I

have been, and I'll never get angry with Paul any more.

MME. DE RÉAN.

I shall add no reprimand nor punishment, Sophie, to that which your own heart has given you. Paul's sufferings are a sufficient punishment for you; you will profit by it far more than by any I could inflict. Moreover, you have been so sincere in confessing your fault when you could have concealed it, that I pardon you also on account of your frankness.

XV.

ELIZABETH.

ONE day, Sophie was quietly seated in her little easy chair, apparently lost in thought. "What are you thinking about?" inquired her mother.

SOPHIE.

I was thinking about Elizabeth Chéneau, mamma.

MME. DE RÉAN.

And thinking what about her?

SOPHIE.

Yesterday, I noticed that she had a great scratch on her arm, and when I asked her how she got it, she blushed, hid her arm, and said to me in a whisper: "Don't speak of it; it was for my punishment." I wonder what she meant by that.

MME. DE RÉAN.

I can explain it to you, if you wish; for I also remarked this scratch, and her mother told me how Elizabeth scratched the arm herself. Pay attention, now, for the act shows a fine trait in Elizabeth.

Sophie, delighted at the thought of hearing a little story, brought her easy chair close to her mother's side the better to catch every word.

MME. DE RÉAN.

You know that Elizabeth is a good child, but unfortunately very high-tempered. (Here Sophie cast her eyes down.) In one of her fits of passion, she even slapped her nurse. She was very sorry for it when the deed was done; but she should have reflected before, instead of afterwards. Day before yesterday she was ironing her doll's underclothing and dresses, her nurse always putting the irons on the fire, for fear Elizabeth would burn herself. Elizabeth was much annoyed at not being allowed to attend to the irons; but Louise (her nurse) positively forbade her doing so, and stopped her every time she attempted to carry out her plan by

SOPHIE'S TROUBLES. 157.

stealth. At last, Elizabeth succeeded in reaching the chimney, but the nurse caught her before she (Elizabeth) could set the iron on the fire. Taking it from her, Louise said, "Since you

will not listen to me, Elizabeth, you iron no more to-day. I shall put the irons in the armoire."—" I want my irons: I want my irons," cried Elizabeth.—" No, you shall not have them."--"You wicked Louise, give me back my irons;" screamed Elizabeth enraged.—"No, you shall not have them; they are locked up," replied Louise, taking the key out of the armoire. Elizabeth, now beside herself with anger, tried to snatch the key from Louise's hand; but finding that she could not she gave Louise's arm such a scratch that it bled. At sight of the blood, Elizabeth's fury vanished; and filled with grief, she begged Louise's pardon, kissed her arm and bathed it in warm water. The latter seeing her so distressed told her that the scratch was of no consequence, and did not hurt. "No, no," said Elizabeth in tears, "I ought to suffer just as I have made you suffer. Scratch my arm, nurse, just as I have scratched yours, so as to make me suffer like you." You know very well that this request was not complied with, and the matter apparently rested there. Elizabeth was very good the remainder of the day; and at night she allowed herself to be put to bed without the least resistance. Next morning, when the nurse took her up, she noticed blood on the sheet, and looking at Elizabeth's arm, she saw that it was terribly scratched. "What has hurt you thus, my poor child?" she exclaimed. "I, I did it, nurse, to punish myself for having scratched you the way I did yesterday. When I went to bed, I thought it only right that I should suffer just as I had made you suffer, and so I scratched my arm until it bled." The nurse much touched at this, embraced Elizabeth, who promised her to be good in future. You understand now the meaning of what Elizabeth said to you, and why she blushed.

SOPHIE.

Oh! yes, mamma, I understand perfectly. It was beautiful in Elizabeth to do that. I should think she would never get angry again, since she knows how wrong it is.

MME. DE RÉAN, (*smiling*).

Do you never do what you know to be wrong?

SOPHIE, (*greatly embarrassed*).

But, mamma, I am younger than she is: I am only four years old, and Elizabeth is five.

MME. DE RÉAN.

That is very little difference in your ages. Remember how angry you were about a week ago, with poor Paul, who is so gentle.

SOPHIE.

Yes, mamma; but I believe, all the same, that I will never behave so again, or do anything that I know to be wrong.

MME. DE RÉAN.

I hope that you will not, Sophie; but take great care not to think yourself better than you are. That is what we call pride, and you know that pride is a very ugly fault.

Sophie made no reply, but a smile of satisfaction that played around her lips, seemed to say that she felt certain she would always be good.

Poor Sophie was soon humiliated, as we shall learn from the following account of what took place two days after.

XVI.

The Conserved Fruits.

SOPHIE had just returned from a walk with her cousin, Paul. They found, waiting in the vestibule, a man who seemed to be a stage driver. He was holding a package under his arm.

"Whom do you wish to see, Sir?" inquired Paul, very politely.

THE MAN.

Mme. De Réan, Monsieur; I have a package for her.

SOPHIE.

Who sent it?

THE MAN.

I do not know, Miss; I have brought it from the stage, and it came from Paris.

SOPHIE.

And what is in it?

THE MAN.

Conserved fruits and apricot paste, I think; at least, that is what it is marked on the stage-book.

Sophie's eyes sparkled, and she passed her tongue over her lips.

"Let us go at once, and tell mamma," said she to Paul, starting off in a run as she uttered the words.

In a few moments, Mme. De Réan appeared, paid the carriage of the package, and brought it into the sitting room, followed by Sophie and Paul. They were both very much surprised and disappointed, when Mme. De Réan, putting the package on the table, quietly resumed her reading and writing.

Sophie and Paul looked at each other with an air of great dissatisfaction.

"Ask mamma to open it," whispered Sophie to Paul.

PAUL, (*whispering*).

I dare not; aunt doesn't like to see any one so impatient and curious.

SOPHIE, (*whispering*).

Ask her, then, if she won't let us open the package to spare her the trouble of doing it.

MME. DE RÉAN.

I hear very well what you say, Sophie. It is ugly and bad in you to be so deceitful, pretending that you wish to be obliging, and spare me trouble by opening the package, when, in reality, your real motives are nothing but curiosity and gluttony. If you had said to me frankly, "Mamma, I am so anxious to see the conserved fruits; won't you please let me undo the package?" I should have said "Yes"; but now, I forbid your touching it.

Sophie, confused and displeased, went to her room, followed by Paul.

"That is what you get by trying to deceive," said Paul. "You are always doing something like that, and you know that aunt detests deception."

SOPHIE.

Why didn t you ask her to let us open the package when I first told you to ask her? You are always setting yourself up for good, and acting nonsense.

PAUL.

First, I don't act nonsense; and, secondly, I don't set up for good. You say that just because you are furious at not tasting any of the conserved fruits.

SOPHIE.

Not at all, Sir; but I am furious at you, because you are always getting me scolded.

PAUL.

Even the day you gave me such a scratching. (Sophie, filled with shame at the recollection, blushed, and said nothing.) Both now remained silent for some time. Sophie longed to beg Paul's pardon, but self-love restrained her; and Paul, who was forgiving, wished also to speak to her, but he did not know how to begin the conversation. At last, he hit upon a clever plan. Balancing himself upon his chair, he leaned back so far that he fell over. Sophie immediately ran to his assistance.

"My poor Paul, are you hurt?" said she.

PAUL.

No; just the contrary.

SOPHIE, (*laughing*).

Just the contrary? That is queer; what do you mean by that?

PAUL.

I mean that my falling over put an end to our quarrel.

SOPHIE, (*embracing him*).

O dear Paul, how good you are! And you fell over on purpose! you might have hurt yourself.

PAUL.

Oh, no. How could any one get hurt falling off a chair as low as this? Now we are friends again, come, let us play.

And together, they started off in a run. In going through the sitting room they saw the package, still unopened. Sophie was very anxious to stop and take another look at it, but Paul pulled her along, and they thought no more about it.

After dinner, Mme. De Réan called the children to her.

"Come, children," said she, "come, we are going to open the wonderful package, and taste some of our conserved fruits. Paul, get me a knife to cut the string." Quick as a flash, Paul disappeared and returned with the knife which he handed his aunt.

Mme. De Réan cut the string, took off the papers enveloping the package, and disclosed to view twelve boxes of conserved fruits and of apricot paste.

"Let us now taste and see how good they are," said she, opening a box. "Take two pieces of fruit, Sophie, whichever you prefer. Here are pears, prunes, nuts, apricots, angelicas, citron."

Sophie, after a little hesitation, looking to see which were the largest, at last, decided upon an apricot and a pear. Paul chose a prune and an angelica. When all three had taken some, mamma shut up the box which was still almost full, took it to her room and put it on the top shelf of an étagère, Sophie following close behind her.

On her return to the sitting room, Mme. De

Réan told Sophie and Paul that she could not take them out walking, she was going to pay a visit in the neighborhood that afternoon.

"Amuse yourselves, children, during my absence," said she; "either play near the house, or take a walk, just as you prefer."

Embracing them, she got in the carriage, with M. and Mme. D'Aubert and M. De Réan.

The two children thus left to themselves, played a long time before the house, Sophie every once in a while, mentioning the conserved fruits.

"I am so sorry," said she, "that I didn't take an angelica, or a prune. They must be delicious."

"Yes, they are delicious," answered Paul; "but you can have some to-morrow; so, don't think anything more about them now, but let us keep on playing."

They continued their sport which was one of Paul's invention—it was to dig out a little basin in the earth, and fill it with water. The water however being soaked up as soon as poured in, they must needs keep on pouring more in. At last, Paul, slipping on the muddy ground, upset a watering-pot all over himself.

"Ugh! ugh!" cried he, "how cold it is! I am soaking; I must go change my shoes, my stockings, and my pantaloons. Wait here for me, Sophie; I'll be back in a quarter of an hour."

Sophie remained near the basin, striking the water with her little shovel, but thinking neither of the water, the shovel, nor Paul. Of what then was she thinking? Alas! of the conserved fruits—the angelicas and the prunes, regretting that she had not eaten some of these too and thus had a taste of all.

"To-morrow," thought she, "mamma will give me some of the fruits again," and I shall not have time then to make a good choice. If I could only look at them beforehand, I could choose what I should like to have to-morrow.... And why shouldn't I look at them now? I have only to open the box."

Delighted at the idea, Sophie ran immediately to her mamma's room to get the box, but she could not reach it. In vain did she jump and stretch out her arm towards it—all in vain. Puzzled, she scarcely knew what to do. Suddenly, whilst looking about for a stick, the tongs—anything to help her reach the box, she suddenly tapped her forehead and exclaimed, "How stupid I am! I can draw an arm-chair up and stand on the top of it!"

She now pushed and dragged close up to the étagère a heavy arm-chair, and climbing thereupon, she reached the box, opened it and looked at the contents with watering mouth. "Which shall I take to-morrow?" thought she. It was very hard for her to make a choice; now, she preferred this, now, that. Time was passing however, and Paul would soon be back.

"What would he think if he were to see me now?" said she to herself. "He would believe that I was stealing the conserved fruits, and yet I am not. I am only looking at them.... Oh! I have a splendid idea! I will nibble a little of each kind of fruit, so as to get the taste of each, and know which is best. No one will be any the wiser for it, because I will take such a tiny bit, that it can't be noticed."

And Sophie nibbled first an angelica, then an apricot, then a prune, a walnut, a pear, a piece of citron but still she could not decide which was best.

"I must begin again," said she.

She suits the action to the word, and begins so many times, that at last, there is scarcely anything left in the box. Perceiving it, she is filled with fright.

"Oh my! oh my! what have I done?" said she. "I wished only to taste the different fruits, and behold I have nearly eaten them up. Mamma will see it as soon as she opens the box and she will suspect me, at once. What shall I do? what shall I do? I could say that I didn't eat them, but mamma won't believe me. Suppose I tell her it was the mice? That is the very thing for me to do· I saw a mouse running along the corridor this morning. I will tell mamma it was a rat that eat them, for a rat is much larger than a mouse, and consequently, eats more, and as I have almost emptied the box, it would be better for me to lay it on a rat than a mouse."

Sophie, delighted with her ingenuity, closed the box, put it back in its place and got down off the chair. She returned to the garden in a run, and had barely time to take her shovel in hand ere Paul made his appearance.

PAUL.

I have been a very long time haven't I? It

was because I couldn't find my shoes; they had been taken away to be cleaned, and I searched all about for them, before asking Baptiste where they were. What were you doing while I was gone?

SOPHIE.

Oh! nothing at all except playing with the water whilst waiting for you.

PAUL.

And you have let the basin get empty; there is no water at all in it. Give me your shovel to beat the ground a little and make it more solid, whilst you run to get some water from the tub.

Sophie went for the water whilst Paul worked at the basin. When she returned, he gave her back her shovel, saying as he did so:

"Your shovel is all sticky, Sophie; it sticks to my fingers. What have you put on it?"

"Nothing," she answered, "nothing at all. I don't know why it should stick so."

And Sophie immediately plunged both her hands into the watering-pot, full of water, perceiving that they too were very sticky.

PAUL.

Why do you plunge your hands in the watering-pot?

SOPHIE, (*embarrassed*).

To see if it is cold.

PAUL, (*laughing*).

How strangely you act since I have returned. One might suppose that you had been doing something wrong.

SOPHIE, (*troubled*).

What could I have done wrong? Just look around, and see if you can find anything wrong. I don't know why you should say that; you always have so many ridiculous ideas.

PAUL.

How angry you are; I was only teasing you. I really didn't think you had done anything wrong, and you needn't look at me so savagely.

Sophie shrugged her shoulders, again took up the watering-pot and emptied it into the basin, the water, as before, being soaked up by the sand. The two children played thus until

That is the garden of the wicked. Let me bring you to the garden of the just. (Page 175).

eight o'clock, their hour for retiring, when their nurses brought them in.

Sophie had a restless, troubled night. She dreamed that she was near a garden from which she was separated by a fence—a garden filled with beautiful flowers, and fruits apparently delicious. She was seeking an entrance to it, when her good angel drew her back, saying to her sadly, "Do not enter there Sophie; do not taste those fruits which look so tempting; but which are in reality, bitter and empoisoned; nor smell those flowers apparently so beautiful, for they too are empoisoned and their odor rank and infectious. This is the garden of evil. Let me lead you to the garden of good."— "But," said Sophie, "the road to the garden of good is so long and rough, whilst that to the other is covered with a find sand which makes it soft to the foot."—"Yes," answered the angel "but the rough road leads to the garden of delights; whilst this leads to a place of suffering and sorrow; everything within this enclosure is bad; even the beings who dwell here are cruel and wicked; they will laugh at your sufferings, they will strive to increase them, tormenting you themselves." Sophie hesitated;

looking at the beautiful garden with its fruits, its flowers, its shaded sandy paths, and then casting a glance at the rugged, arid road, apparently without end, she snatched her hand from the good angel, and entered the garden. The angel cried to her, "Return, return, Sophie, I will wait for you at the gate; I will wait here until your death; and if ever you return to me, I will lead you into the garden of delight by that rugged road which will grow less rough and more beautiful the farther you advance on it." Sophie did not heed the words of her good angel. Some pretty children beckoning her to come to them, she hastened to join them; and immediately they surrounded her, some pinching her, some pulling her about, and others throwing sand in her eyes.

With difficulty, she got rid of them, and going off some distance, she plucked a flower, which was most beautiful to look upon. Smelling it she threw it far from her—the odor was horrible. Continuing to advance, and seeing trees laden with the richest fruits, she reached forth her hand and taking one of them tasted it; but she cast it from her with even more horror than she did the flower—the taste of it was bitter and detestable. Sophie, continued her walk, growing sadder and sadder; for

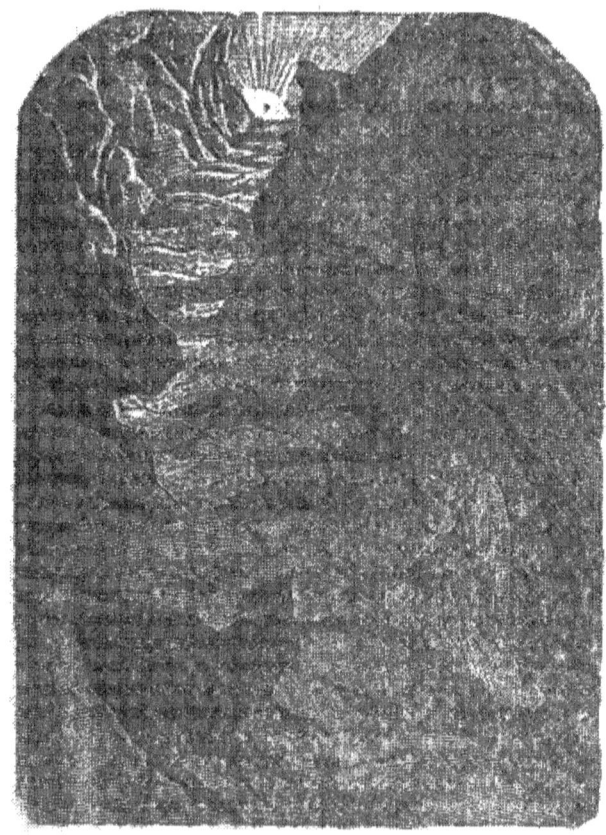

everywhere and in everything here was she deceived, even as she had been by the flowers and the fruits. After remaining in the garden of evil some time, she thought of her good angel, and despite the promises and the cries of the wicked who dwelt herein, she ran to the gate, and there perceived her good angel who extended his hand to her. Repulsing the wicked children, she cast herself into the arms of the angel who hastened to conduct her to the rough road. The first steps on it were very difficult to her; but in proportion as they advanced, the road became smoother, the country through which it passed, more delightful. Just as she was about to enter the garden of good, Sophie awoke, greatly excited and bathed in perspiration. She lay awake a long time pondering this dream. "I must tell mamma," said she, "and ask her to explain it to me." After this, she fell asleep and did not awake until morning.

Mamma's countenance was far from reassuring when Sophie sought her; but the dream had so engrossed the little girl's thoughts that the conserved fruits were forgotten, for the time, and she immediately related the wonderful dream to her mother.

MME. DE RÉAN.

Do you know what this means, Sophie? It means that the good God, who sees how bad you are, warns you by this dream, that if you continue to do wrong because it seems agreeable to you, grief instead of happiness will surely be yours. This garden of deceits is hell; the garden of good is paradise which we reach by a rough road; that is, by refraining from things that are agreeable, but forbidden us. This road is easier to us the longer we keep in it; in other words, by force of long striving to be obedient, gentle, good, we, at last, become so habitually thus, that it no longer costs us to obey and to be good, and we do not suffer from having to curb our will and desires."

Sophie moved about uneasily on her chair; she blushed and looked at her mother; she longed to speak, but she could not make up her mind to do so. At last, Mme De Réan who noticed her agitation came to her aid, by saying;

"Sophie, you have something to confess, and you keep it back, because it is humiliating. It always costs us something to acknowledge our faults. Now, this confession of them is the rough road which your good angel calls you to enter upon, and which seems to frighten you so. Listen to your good angel, and strike out boldly with him on the rough road he now points out to you."

Poor Sophie blushed worse than ever, and hiding her face in her hands, she told her mother in a trembling voice, that the day before she had eaten nearly all the conserved fruits.

MME. DE RÉAN.

And how did you hope to conceal it from me?

SOPHIE.

I intended to tell you, mamma, that the rats had eaten them.

MME. DE RÉAN.

And I should never have believed it, you may rest assured; for rats could not take the cover off a box and put it on again as you have done. They would have gnawed through the box to get at the fruits. Moreover, rats had no need of dragging an arm-chair to help them reach the étagère.

SOPHIE, (*surprised*).

What, mamma! you saw that I had drawn up the arm-chair?

MME. DE RÉAN.

Yes, because you forgot to remove it; it was the first thing that struck me on entering the room. I knew that it was you, especially, after I looked in the box and found it nearly empty. You see now, Sophie, that it has been better for you to acknowledge your fault to me as you have done, than to have concealed it, as lies would only have made things worse, and have increased your punishment. In consideration of the great effort this confession has cost you, and to encourage you always to confess your wrong doings, your only punishment for eating the conserves shall be, to have no more of them as long as the box lasts.

Sophie, kissing the hand of her mamma who embraced her affectionately, now went to her room, where Paul was waiting for her to come to their breakfast.

PAUL.

What is the matter, Sophie, that your eyes are so red?

SOPHIE.

I have been crying.

PAUL.

Why? Has aunt scolded you?

SOPHIE.

No; I have been crying, because I was ashamed at telling mamma something bad that I did yesterday.

PAUL.

Something bad? I don't know of anything bad you did.

SOPHIE.

No, because I kept it from you.

Sophie now told Paul how she had eaten the conserved fruits, after intending only to look at them, and to make a selection for the next day.

Paul praised her very much for having made a full confession of it to her mother.

"How did you have the courage to do so?" he asked.

Sophie then related her dream, and mamma's interpretation of it. Henceforth, the dream was a frequent topic of Paul's and Sophie's conversations, and it aided them greatly in their efforts to be obedient and good.

XVII.

THE CAT AND THE BULLFINCH.

SOPHIE and Paul were one day returning with their nurse, from a walk to the house of a poor woman, to whom they had taken some money. They did not hurry home, but pleasantly sauntered along at their ease, somtimes, one or the other of the children, or may be both, attempting to climb a tree, or crossing the hedges and hiding behind the bushes. Sophie had hidden thus, and Paul was trying to find her, when suddenly she heard, quite near her, a very faint, plaintive *miaou, miaou*. Filled with fright, she ran out from her hiding-place.

"Paul," said she, "let us call nurse: I have just now heard, very near me in the bush, a low cry, like a cat."

PAUL.

Why should we call nurse for that? Let us go ourselves to see what it is.

SOPHIE.

Oh! no, I am afraid.

PAUL, (*laughing*).

Afraid! and of what? You say yourself that it was a faint cry, so, it can't be a big animal.

SOPHIE.

I don't know what it is; it might be a snake, or, a young wolf.

PAUL, (*laughing*).

Ha! ha! ha! a snake that cries! that would certainly be something new! And the idea of a young wolf crying so low that I, who was very near you, didn't even hear it—it is ridiculous!

SOPHIE.

There it is again! Don't you hear it?

Paul listened, and did hear a most feeble *miaou*, coming apparently from something in the bush. Despite Sophie's remonstrances, he ran immediately towards it.

"It's a poor little kitten," said he, after a few moments' search, "that seems sick. Just come see how miserable looking it is."

Sophie ran to the bush, and there all stretched out under it, she saw a poor little white kitten, wet with dew and covered with mud.

"We must call nurse," said she, "to take it up, and carry it for us; poor little thing, how it trembles!"

"And how thin it is!" added Paul.

They called the nurse who was some distance behind. When she had reached them, they showed her the kitten, and asked her to carry it home for them.

NURSE.

But how shall I do it? The miserable little creature is so wet and dirty that I can't take it in my hands.

SOPHIE.

Oh! can't you put it on some leaves, nurse?

PAUL.

Or, in my handkerchief—that would be better.

SOPHIE.

That is the very thing, Paul! let us wipe it off with my handkerchief, and lay it in yours for nurse to carry it.

With the nurse's assistance, they succeeded in drying and cleansing the kitten which had hardly strength to move. Then it was carefully wrapped up in the handkerchief, and the nurse carrying it, they all three hastened to the house to give it some warm milk.

As they were not far from home, it took them a very little while to get there. Sophie and Paul ran on ahead to the kitchen.

"Please, give me a glass of warm milk, right away," said Sophie to John the cook.

"What for, Miss?" he answered.

"For a poor little kitten we found in a hedge, and which is almost starved to death. Here it is; nurse has brought it wrapped up in a handkerchief. The nurse now laid the hand kerchief on the ground; and the cook set a plateful of warm milk before the kitten, which immediately began to lap it up, and continued until there was not a drop left."

"I hope it feels satisfied," said the nurse,

"for it has drunk more than two glasses of milk."

SOPHIE.

Oh! see, it is getting up! it is licking its hair!

PAUL.

Suppose we take it to our room.

THE COOK.

No, my young gentleman, and my young lady, I advise you to leave it in the kitchen; first, because, its coat will dry better in the warm ashes, and it can have something to eat here, as often as it wants to eat; and moreover, it can go out of the kitchen itself whenever it chooses, and thus learn good habits.

PAUL.

That is true. Let us leave it in the kitchen, Sophie.

SOPHIE.

But if I do leave it, will it still be ours, and shall I be able to see it as much as I please?

THE COOK.

Certainly, Miss, it will be yours all the same, and you can see it just whenever you feel like it.

They took the kitten and lay it on the warm ashes under the stove. Leaving it there that it might get a good sleep, the children retired from the kitchen, after strongly urging the cook to put some warm milk close by, for it to get a little whenever it felt hungry.

SOPHIE.

What shall we name our kitten?

PAUL.

Let us call it *Cheri*.

SOPHIE.

Oh! no, that is too common. Suppose we call it *Charmant*.

PAUL.

And what if it should grow up ugly?

SOPHIE.

So it might, and what could we call it, then? We must give it a name.

PAUL.

Do you know what I think would be a very pretty name? *Beau-Minon.*

SOPHIE.

Oh, yes! that is the very name, *Beau-Minon,* as in the Connt De Blondine![1] I am going to ask mamma to make it a little collar, with the name *Beau-Minon* embroidered on it.

And the children hastened to Mme. De Réan, to tell her about the kitten, and ask for its collar. She went to see it and took the measure of its neck.

"I scarcely believe," said she, "this poor little kitten will live. It is so thin and weak that it can hardly stand up."

PAUL.

How could it have got in the hedge? Cats don't live in the woods.

MME. DE RÉAN.

Perhaps it was carried off by some bad children who after playing with it, threw it in

[1] See *Nouveaux Contes De Fées,* (New Fairy Tales), by the same authoress, Mme. De Segur.

the hedge, thinking it could get back to the house by itself.

SOPHIE.

And why didn't it go? It is truly its own fault that it has suffered so.

MME. DE RÉAN.

It is too young to be able to find its way; and perhaps its home was very far off. If some wicked persons were to carry you a great ways from home, and leave you in the woods, do you think you could find your way back alone?

SOPHIE.

Oh! I should not be troubled at all; I should walk straight on until I met somebody, or, come to a house; then I should tell my name, and ask to be taken back home.

MME. DE RÉAN.

You might come across bad, or, at least, disobliging people, who would not be willing to go out of their way, or leave their work, to take you back home. And, moreover, you can speak, thus making one understand what you want. But you know the poor kitten cannot make known its desires, or where it lives. It would be chased off, beaten, killed perhaps.

SOPHIE.

But why did it stay in the bush to die of hunger?

MME. DE RÉAN.

Perhaps some bad boys threw it there, after beating it. However, its staying in the bush proved not such a stupid thing, after all, since you, passing by, saved it.

PAUL.

But, aunt, it couldn't foresee that we were to go by.

MME. DE RÉAN.

The kitten itself could not, but the good God did; and He permitted it to remain there to give you an opportunity of practising charity even towards an animal.

Sophie and Paul, who were impatient to see their kitten again, made no reply, but returned to the kitchen, where they found *Beau-Minon* sound asleep on the warm ashes, with a little bowl of milk beside it, placed there by the cook. As there was nothing now to be done for their pet, the two children ran out to play in their garden.

Beau-Minon did not die; in a very short time, he was strong, well, and lively. His beauty increased with his growth; his long white hair was soft and silky; his big black eyes gleamed like the sun; and his pink nose gave him a gentle, infantive expression. He was a real Angora cat, of the most beautiful species. Sophie loved him much, and so did Paul, who frequently spent a few days with Sophie. *Beau-Minon* was the happiest of cats. He had one fault, however, which grieved his mistress very much—he was so cruel to the birds. No sooner was he out of doors, than he would climb up the trees, hunting birds' nests, and eating the little ones he found in them. Sometimes, he would eat even the poor mother birds, striving to defend their young against him. When Sophie and Paul saw him climbing up trees, they would do everything in their power to make him come down, but all in vain; *Beau-Minon* paid no attention to them; he continued his mischievous course all the same, eating the little birds whenever he could. And oh! such plaintive cries of *quee, quee,* as would then be heard.

On these occasions, when *Beau-Minon* descended the tree, Sophie would sting him well with a switch. *Beau-Minon,* after a while, however, found means of avoiding this: sometimes, by staying up the tree so long that Sophie got tired waiting for him; or, again, by coming half way down, then springing to the ground at a little distance from her, and running away so fast that she could not catch him.

"Take care, *Beau-Minon,*" the children would say, "the good God will punish you for your cruelty. One day, something will happen to you."

The warning was lost on *Beau-Minon,* for he never even listened to it.

One day, Mme. De Réan brought into the sitting room, a charming bird, in a pretty gilded cage.

"See, children," said she, "what a pretty bullfinch one of my friends has sent me. He sings delightfully."

SOPHIE AND PAUL, (*together*).

Oh! how I should love to hear him.

MME. DE RÉAN.

I am going to make him sing, but don't come too near the cage, lest you frighten him.

"Little one, little one," she continued, speaking now to the bird, "sing, dear, sing, little one, sing."

The bullfinch, poising himself, and inclining his head, first to one side, then, to the other, now began to whistle the air: *By the light of the moon*. Finishing this, he treated them to another: *I have some good tobacco;* and again, another: *The good king Dagobert*.

The children listened motionless; they scarcely dared to breathe lest they should frighten the bird. When it had finished, Paul exclaimed, "Oh! aunt, how he sings! What a sweet voice he has! I could listen to him forever!"

"We will make him sing again, after dinner," said Mme. De Réan. "He is tired now, from his long journey. We must give him something to eat. Go to the garden, children, and get me some chickweed or some plaintain. The gardener will show you where to find them."

Paul and Sophie ran to the kitchen-garden and returned with enough chickweed to bury the cage in. Mme. De Réan told them that next time, they must not bring more than a

handful. They put some of it in the cage, and the bullfinch immediately began to peck at it.

"Let us go to dinner now, children," said Mme. De Réan. "Your papas are waiting for us."

The pretty bullfinch was the subject of conversation during dinner.

"What a beautiful black head he has!" said Sophie.

PAUL.

And such a beautiful red breast!"

MME. DE RÉAN.

How delightfully he sings.

M. DE RÉAN.

We must make him sing all his airs.

As soon as dinner was over, they all repaired to the sitting room, the children running ahead. As they entered the room, Mme. De Réan heard them shriek, and hastening to see what was the matter, she beheld them motionless from fright, and pointing towards the bullfinch's cage. From this cage, several bars of which were bent and broken, *Beau-Minon* had just jumped down, holding in his mouth, the poor bullfinch, its wings still fluttering. Mme. De Réan screamed in turn, and ran at *Beau-Minon* to make him drop the bird; but the culprit took refuge under an arm-chair. M. De Réan, who now entered the room, seized the tongs and tried to hit *Beau-Minon,* but the latter, ever on the alert, darted through the open door, M. De Réan pursuing him from room to room, from corridor to corridor. The poor bird now cried no longer, nor did it struggle. Finally, M. De Réan succeeded in hitting *Beau-Minon* with the tongs, but such a blow that the cat's mouth opened, and the bird dropped from it, one falling to one side,

and one to the other. After two or three convulsions, *Beau-Minon* did not stir—the tongs had struck him in the head, he was dead.

Mme. De Réan and the children who ran after M. De Réan in his pursuit of the cat and the bullfinch, came up just as *Beau-Minon* had his last convulsion.

" *Beau-Minon!* my poor *Beau-Minon!*" cried Sophie, greatly distressed.

"The bullfinch, the bullfinch!" cried Paul.

"My dear, what have you done?" exclaimed Mme. De Réan.

"I have punished the guilty," replied he, "but without saving the innocent. The bullfinch is dead, strangled by wicked *Beau-Minon* that will never kill anything again, since I have killed him, without intending it!"

Sophie dared not make any reply; but she wept bitterly over the death of her cat, loving him much, in spite of his faults.

"I spoke truly," said Paul, "when I told *Beau-Minon* that the good God would punish him for his wickedness to the birds. Alas! poor *Beau-Minon,* you are dead, and it is all your own fault!"

XVIII.

The Work Box.

WHEN Sophie saw anything she wished to have, she would ask for it. If her mother refused her, she would keep on asking, until, at last, Mme. De Réan, tired of being annoyed would send her to her room. There, instead of banishing the thought, Sophie would continue to brood over it, repeating to herself:

"How can I manage to get what I want? I am so anxious to have it! I must try to get it somehow."

And very often her efforts to carry out her determination resulted in a punishment; still, she did not correct this fault.

One day, her mamma called her to show her a beautiful work-box that M. De Réan had just sent from Paris. The outside was covered with a layer of thin gold, and the inside lined with blue velvet. It contained every article that the best appointed work-box could have, and all of gold—thimble, scissors, a little sheath, a stilletto, bobbins, a knife, pen-knife, nippers, a bodkin. In another compartment were a box of needles, one of gilt pins, and an assortment of silk of all colors, thread of different sizes, tapes, ribbons etc. Sophie uttered an exclamation of delight at seeing all these things.

Oh! oh! how pretty they are!" said she, "and how very convenient to have everything that one needs for her work! Whose box is this, mamma?" she added, smiling, as if sure the answer would be, " *It is yours.*"

"Your papa sent it to me," was the reply.

SOPHIE.

What a pity! I am so sorry! I should love so to have it.

MME. DE RÉAN.

Well, really! I thank you! And you are sorry because this pretty box is mine! That is a little selfish, Sophie.

SOPHIE.

Oh! mamma, give it to me, please do give it to me.

MME. DE RÉAN.

You do not sew well enough yet to have such a pretty box. Moreover, you are not sufficiently orderly. You would keep nothing in its place, and you would be sure to lose or mislay, one after another, everything in the box.

SOPHIE.

Oh! no, mamma, I assure you, I would not; I would be so very careful.

MME. DE RÉAN.

No, no, Sophie, you are too young to have it; so, think no more about it.

SOPHIE.

Mamma, I am beginning to sew very well. I am fond of sewing.

MME. DE RÉAN.

Ah, indeed! Then why are you always vexed when I make you do it?

SOPHIE, (*embarrassed.*)

Because.... because.... I haven't everything I need for my work. But if I just had this box, I could work with pleasure, . . . oh! such pleasure.

MME. DE RÉAN.

Try to take pleasure in your work, without having the box; this may be the means of your getting one.

SOPHIE.

Oh! mamma, please give it to me.

MME. DE RÉAN.

Sophie, you annoy me. I tell you to think no more about the box.

Sophie made no reply, but she continued looking at the coveted object, and, in a short time, commenced begging for it again. Her mother growing impatient now sent her into the garden.

But even out in the garden, Sophie would neither play nor walk about. Seated upon a bench, she still dwelt upon the coveted box, and tried to devise some means of getting it.

"If I knew how to write," said she, "I should write to papa to send me one just like that; but I can't write; and if I were to die,

tate such a letter to mamma, she would only scold me, and not write the letter. I could wait until papa returned, but that would be too long, and I want the box now."

Sophie sat thinking a long, long time; at last she jumped up from the bench clapped her hands together and exclaimed!

"I have it! I have it! the box is mine!"

And immediately she returned to the room where it had been left. It was on the table, and she saw no one about. She advanced cautiously, opened the box, and one by one, took everything out of it. Her heart beat violently, for she was stealing, just like the thieves that are put in prison; and she was afraid some one might enter the room, ere she had finished. But no one did come, and she was thus able to rifle the box of all its contents. Gently closing it, she replaced it in the middle of the table, and went to the room where her playthings and furniture were. Opening the drawer of her little table, she there carefully stowed away all that she had just stolen.

"There, now," said she, "when mamma finds she has only an empty box, she will be very willing to give it to me. I can then replace everything as it was before, and the pretty work-box will really be mine!"

Delighted at the hope, Sophie felt not the least self-reproach for what she had done; nor did she either ask herself: " What will mamma say? Whom will she accuse of having stolen her things? What answer can I make if she asks me whether I did it?" No, she thought of nothing except her happiness in possessing the box.

The whole morning passed without Mme. De Réan's discovering Sophie's theft; but just about dinner time, when the family were assembled in the parlor, she (Mme. De Réan) told some friends who had been invited to dine with her, that she was going to show them a most beautiful little work-box which M. De Réan had sent her from Paris.

"You will see," she added, "how complete it is; it contains every article that could possibly be needed for one's work. Look first at the exterior of the box; is'nt it pretty?"

She now opened it to display the contents. Imagine her astonishment and that of all her friends to find it empty!

"What's the meaning of this?" she exclaimed. "Everything was in place this morning, and I have not touched it since."

"Did you leave it in the parlor?" asked one of the ladies, an invited guest.

MME. DE RÉAN.

Certainly, and without a shadow of fear; all my servants are honest, and incapable of stealing from me.

THE LADY.

But, my dear madame, as the box is empty, it is very certain that some one must have emptied it.

Sophie's heart beat violently during this conversation; and she kept herself in the back-ground, trembling in every limb, and her face as red as a radish.

Mme De Réan, glancing around for her, and not seeing her, called:

"Sophie, Sophie, where are you?"

As Sophie did not answer, the ladies, behind whom she had sought to conceal herself, perceiving this, stepped aside, and Sophie appeared, suffused with blushes, and in such a state of confusion, that no one present had much doubt as to who was the thief.

"Come here, Sophie," said Mme. De Réan.

Sophie came, but very slowly, her limbs trembling under her.

MME. DE RÉAN.

Where have you put the things which were in my box?

SOPHIE, (*trembling*).

Indeed, mamma, I haven't taken anything, I haven't hidden anything.

MME. DE RÉAN.

It is useless for you to lie, Miss; bring me, this minute, everything you have taken, if you don't wish to be punished as you deserve.

SOPHIE, *(crying)*.

But, mamma, I assure you, I haven't taken anything.

MME. DE RÉAN.

Follow me, Miss.

As Sophie did not budge, Mme. De Réan took her by the hand, and pulled her along to the play-room, despite her resistance. Mme.

SOPHIE'S TROUBLES. 213

De Réan now searched Sophie's little chest of drawers, and the doll's armoire. Finding nothing, she began to think that she had done the child a great injustice. She next went to-

wards the little table; and Sophie's heart beat faster, and her limbs trembled worse than ever, when her mamma, opening the drawer, beheld every article that had been stolen from the work-box.

Without saying one word, Mme. De Réan gave Sophie such a whipping as she had never given her before. In vain did Sophie cry, and beg her mother to spare her—all in vain. She was whipped severely, and we must say that she deserved it.

Emptying the drawer of its contents, Mme. De Réan returned to the parlor, and replaced them in the box, leaving Sophie weeping bitterly, all alone in the play-room.

Sophie was so ashamed that she would not go into dinner. And it was just as well that she did not; for Mme. De Réan, after a while, sent the nurse to take her to her own (Sophie's) room, there to dine and spend the evening. Sophie cried long and bitterly. Even the nurse, notwithstanding, her habitual indulgence to Sophie, was indignant at the theft, and called her a thief.

"I must lock everything up," said she, "for fear you steal from me. If anything is lost in this house hereafter, we shall know where to find the thief, and we will go straight to your drawers to search them."

Next day, Mme. De Réan had Sophie brought to her, and read her the following letter.

"Listen, Miss, to what your papa wrote when he sent me the box," said Mme. De Réan.

"I have just bought a lovely work-box, my dear, which I send you. It is for Sophie; but do not tell her this, nor give it to her yet. Let it be the reward of a week's good behavior. Let her see the box, but do not say I bought it for her, as I wish her to be good, not from interested motives, the hope of obtaining thus a handsome present, but from the true desire alone of doing what is right."

"You see," continued Mme. De Réan, "that in stealing from me, you were stealing from yourself. After what you have done, you shall never have the box, even if you were to be good for a month. I hope, now, that you will profit by this lesson, and never more be guilty of anything so bad and shameful."

Sophie cried bitterly again, and implored her mamma's forgiveness, which Mme. De Réan at last accorded her, telling her, however, that she should never have the box.

Some time after this, it was given to little Elizabeth Chêneau, who sewed beautifully for her years, and was a remarkably good child.

When honest little Paul learned what Sophie had done, he, too, was so indignant that he did not visit her for a week. Hearing afterwards, however, that she was very much grieved at her fault, and thoroughly repentant, and how mortified she was at being called a thief, his heart was deeply touched. He went to see her, and instead of reproaching, he did his best to console her.

"My poor Sophie," said he, "do you know how to make every one forget your theft? It is to be so honest, that no one can ever again even have a suspicion against you."

Sophie promised Paul to be very honest, and she ever after kept her word.

XIX.

The Donkey.

SOPHIE had been very good for two weeks, not having committed any great fault during all that time. Paul said he had not seen her angry for a long while, and the nurse said that she had become obedient. Mme. De Réan also observed that Sophie was no longer gluttonous, untruthful, nor lazy. She wished to reward her, but did not know what reward would be the most acceptable.

One day, while sewing near the open window, she overheard a conversation between Sophie and Paul, playing in front of the house, which gave her the desired information.

PAUL, (*wiping his face*).

How warm I am! How warm I am! I am all in a perspiration!

SOPHIE, (*doing the same*).

And I also! Yet, we have not got through with much work.

PAUL.

That is because our wheelbarrows are so small.

SOPHIE.

If we were to take the big kitchen-garden wheelbarrows, we would get along faster with our work.

PAUL.

We haven't the strength to wheel them. One day, I attempted to use one; I had great difficulty even to raise it, and when I tried to advance, the weight of it drew me to one side, and I upset all the earth that was in the barrow.

SOPHIE.

Our garden will never be finished; before spading and planting it, we shall have to put on it more than a hundred wheelbarrows of rich earth. And we have so far to go for it!

PAUL.

We can't help that. It will take us a long time, but we will get through.

SOPHIE.

Oh! if we had only a donkey, like Camille and Madeleine De Fleurville, and a little cart, we could get through with our work in a very little while.

PAUL.

Indeed we could! but as we haven't one, we must do the work of a donkey ourselves.

SOPHIE.

Listen to me, Paul, I have an idea.

PAUL, (*laughing*).

Oh! if you have an idea, we are sure to do some mischief, for your ideas are generally not famous of their sort.

SOPHIE, (*with impatience*).

But do listen to me, before you begin to make fun. My idea is excellent. How much spending money does aunt give you a week?

PAUL.

A franc, but part of it is for the poor.

SOPHIE.

Good! I also get a franc a week; so, between us we have two francs a week. Now, instead of spending our money let us keep it until we have enough to buy a donkey and cart.

PAUL.

That would really be a good idea, if instead of two francs we had twenty; but with only two francs we should have to keep ourselves the alms we have been giving the poor, which would not be right, and then wait two years before we could save up enough to buy a donkey and cart.

SOPHIE.

Two francs a week would be how much a month?

PAUL.

I don't know exactly what it would amount to, but I know it is very little.

SOPHIE, (*after reflecting*).

Oh! I have another idea. Let us ask mamma and aunt to give us the money they would spend for our New Year's gifts.

PAUL.

They would not do it.

SOPHIE.

Let us keep on asking them.

PAUL.

You ask your mamma, if you wish to do it; but I prefer waiting to hear what answer she gives you; and I will not ask unless she tells you yes.

Sophie ran immediately to her mother, who of course, never intimated that she had heard the conversation. "Mamma," said she, "will you give me my New Year's gift in advance."

MME. DE BÉAN.

Your New Year's gift? I cannot buy it here. It is only on our return from Paris that I shall have it.

SOPHIE.

Oh! I mean the money, mamma, that you would spend for it. I want the money so much.

MME. DE RÉAN.

How can you be so in need of money? if it is for the poor, tell me; and I will give you what is necessary, for you know I never refuse you anything for the poor.

SOPHIE, (*embarrassed*).

No, mamma, it is not for the poor; it is. . . . it is. . . to buy a donkey with.

MME. DE RÉAN.

What would you do with a donkey?

SOPHIE.

Oh! we need one so much, mamma—we really do, Paul and I. Just see how warm I am, and Paul is even warmer than I am. It is because we have been wheeling the rich earth to our garden.

MME. DE RÉAN, (*laughing*).

And do you believe that a donkey would wheel it for you?

SOPHIE.

Oh! no mamma, I know a donkey couldn't do that, I haven't told you yet that with the donkey, we should also like to have a little cart. We could harness our donkey to the cart, and in this way haul a great deal of earth at once, without being so fatigued as we now are, bringing a little at a time.

MME. DE RÉAN.

I acknowledge that your idea is a good one.
SOPHIE, (*clapping her hands*).
Ah! I knew very well that it was good. . . . Paul, Paul," she continued, calling from the window.

MME. DE RÉAN.

Wait now before rejoicing. Your idea is good, but I do not intend to give you the money.

SOPHIE, (*in dismay*).

But what then are we to do?

MME. DE RÉAN.

Don't worry about it, but keep perfectly quiet, and be very good, so as to merit the donkey and little wagon, that I am going to buy you as soon as possible.

SOPHIE, (*throwing herself upon her mother's neck and embracing her*).

Oh! what a happiness! what a happiness; Thanks, dear mamma. Paul....Paul....we have a donkey....we have a little wagon.... Come here, come quick!

PAUL, (*running*).

Where? where? where are they?

SOPHIE.

Mamma gives them to us; she is going to buy them for us.

MME. DE RÉAN.

Yes, I give them to both of you: to you Paul, as a reward for your kindness to those around you, your obedience, your general good behavior; to you, Sophie, as an incentive to imitate your cousin, and an encouragement to continue as gentle, obedient, industrious as you have been the last two weeks. Come with me to hunt Lambert; we will explain the matter to him, and commission him to buy the donkey and cart.

The two children did not wait to be told a second time, but ran on ahead of Mme. De Réan. Lambert they found in the yard, measuring some oats which he had just bought. Both began talking to him at once, and in such a state of happy excitement, that it was impossible for him to comprehend their meaning. He stood looking at them in astonishment, when Mme. De Réan, now came up, and, in a few words, made known to him her wishes.

SOPHIE.

Go at once, Lambert, I beg of you; for we must have our donkey right off, before dinner.

LAMBERT, (*laughing*).

A donkey can't be picked up as easily a stick, Miss. I must look around in the neighborhood, first, to ascertain whether there is one for sale; and then, I must see to it that he is very gentle, that he does not kick, nor bite, that he is not obstinate, and neither too old nor too young.

SOPHIE.

Oh! my, my gracious! how many qualities you expect in a donkey! Take the first one you find, Lambert; that will be the quickest way.

LAMBERT.

No, Miss, I shall not take the first I come across; this would be exposing you to be bitten or kicked

SOPHIE.

Bah! bah! Paul knows well how to manage a donkey and make him behave.

PAUL.

Not at all; I should not be willing to drive a biting, kicking donkey.

MME. DE RÉAN.

Leave it in Lambert's hands. You see that your commission will be well attended to. He knows what he is about, and he will take every pains.

PAUL.

And the wagon, aunt? How can we get one small enough for the donkey to draw?

LAMBERT.

Don't bother about that, Mr. Paul; whilst waiting to have your wagon made, I will lend you my big dog-cart, which you may keep just as long as you please.

PAUL.

Oh! thanks, Lambert; that will be delightful.

SOPHIE.

Oh! Lambert, do start right off.

MME. DE RÉAN.

You must give him time to put away his oats; if he leaves them in the yard, they will be eaten up by the chickens and the birds.

Seeing the children's impatience, Lambert stowed the bags of oats away in the barn, and immediately started out in search of a donkey.

Sophie and Paul believing that he would return very promptly bringing the animal, remained just in front of the house waiting for him, from time to time, going to the yard to see if he had come. In about an hour, they began to grow weary of this.

PAUL, (*yawning*).

Sophie, what do you say to our going to play in our garden?

SOPHIE, (*yawning*).

Are we not amusing ourselves here?

PAUL, (*yawning*).

It doesn't seem so to me. For my part, I am not being amused at all, I find this waiting very tiresome.

SOPHIE.

And if we leave here we shall miss seeing Lambert come with the donkey.

PAUL.

I begin to think that he is not coming very soon.

SOPHIE.

And I think just the contrary.

PAUL.

Let us wait a little then; but, (he continued, yawning,) it is so very tiresome.

SOPHIE.

Go then if you are tired; I don't ask you to stay here, I can stay by myself.

PAUL, (*after a little hesitation*).

Well, I believe I will go; it is too stupid to lose all day waiting. And what good does it do to wait? If Lambert brings the donkey we shall know it immediately, for some one will come at once to our garden to tell us—you know very well they will. And if he doesn't bring it, tell me what good there would be in our waiting?

SOPHIE.

Go, Sir, go; I don't prevent you.

PAUL.

Ah! bah! You are in a pout without knowing why. Good-bye then, until dinner, Miss grumbler.

SOPHIE.

Good-bye, Mr. ill-mannered, sullen, disagreeable, impertinent.

PAUL, (*with a gesture of mockery*).

Good-bye sweet, patient, amiable Sophie.

Sophie ran towards Paul to slap him, but he foreseeing this, had already started off, just as fast as his legs could take him. Looking back to see whether she was pursuing him, he saw that she was, and with a stick that she had picked up. Paul outran her and hid himself in the woods. Sophie now losing sight of him returned to her station before the house.

"Oh! how thankful I am," thought she, "that Paul ran and I did not overtake him, for I should have hit him with the stick and hurt him; mamma would have known it, and then she would not have given me my donkey, nor the little cart. When Paul comes, I will embrace him... He is so good... but a great tease for all that."

Sophie remained before the house, waiting for Lambert, until the dinner bell rang.

She went in, much displeased at having waited so long in vain. Paul, who found her in her room, looked mockingly at her.

"Did you have a nice time?" said he.

SOPHIE.

No; I was tired out waiting, and you were right not to stay. That Lambert is not back yet. Oh! it is so worrying!

PAUL.

I told you so.

SOPHIE.

Yes, I know you did; but it is none the less tiresome and worrying, for all that.

Just then there was a rap at the door. The nurse answered, "Come in." The door opened, and Lambert appeared. Sophie and Paul uttered a cry of joy.

"The donkey? The donkey?" they both inquired at once.

LAMBERT.

There is not a donkey for sale anywhere about, Miss. Ever since I left you, I have been on the hunt for one, going every place in the neighborhood that I thought there was a probability of my finding one, but all in vain.

SOPHIE, (*in tears*).

Oh! how unfortunate! how unfortunate! What shall we do?

LAMBERT.

Don't be so distressed, Miss; we will surely get one, but we may have to wait a little.

PAUL.

How long do you think?

LAMBERT.

A week, perhaps, or a fortnight; I can't say exactly how long; that depends on circumstances. To-morrow, I go to the town-market, and I may come across a jenny there.

PAUL.

A jenny! What is that—a jenny?

LAMBERT.

You, who are so knowing, don't know what a jenny is? Why, it is a donkey.

SOPHIE.

A jenny! that is a funny name! I never heard it before.

LAMBERT.

Ah, Miss! we learn as we grow older. I must find your mamma, to tell her that early to-morrow morning, I am going to the market to try and get the jenny. Good-bye, Mr. Paul and Miss Sophie.

And Lambert went out, leaving the children much disappointed at not having their donkey.

"We may have to wait a long time," said they, sighing.

The next morning, they passed in anxious expectation. In vain did Mme. De Réan tell them that it was nearly always thus; that it was impossible to get just what one wanted, and at the moment; that we must school ourselves to waiting, and even sometimes to the discipline of never getting what we had long hoped for. The children would answer, "Yes, that is so," but they sighed none the less, and none the less impatiently watched for the return of Lambert with a donkey. At last, Paul, who was at the window, thought that he heard at a distance, the hi hau! hi hau! of a donkey.

"Sophie, Sophie," cried he, "listen. Don't you hear a donkey braying? Perhaps Lambert is coming."

MME. DE RÉAN.

Perhaps it is a donkey in the neighborhood, or one passing along the road.

SOPHIE.

Oh! please, mamma, let me go see if it isn't Lambert with the jenny?

MME. DE RÉAN.

The jenny? What manner of speaking is that? It is only the rough peasantry who call a donkey by that name.

PAUL.

Aunt, that is what Lambert called it; and he was even astonished that we didn't know what he meant.

MME. DE RÉAN.

Lambert uses the language of his own class of people; but you, who live amidst educated and refined people, must not speak thus.

SOPHIE.

Oh! indeed, mamma, I still hear the hi hau! hi hau! of a donkey; may we go see where it is?

MME. DE RÉAN.

Yes, go, children, go; but only to the big road: don't pass the gate.

Away sped Sophie and Paul like arrows. Mme. De Réan called out to them:

"Don't go through the grass, it is too high:

nor through the woods, on account of the briers!"

But they did not hear her, and went bounding like deer over the grass and through the woods, to shorten their way. They soon reached the fence, and the first thing they saw on the big road, was Lambert, leading by a halter a superb donkey, not too large, however.

"The donkey! The donkey! Thanks, Lambert, thanks! Oh! how delightful!" they both exclaimed at once.

"How pretty he is!" said Paul.

"How good he looks!" said Sophie. "Let us go at once to tell mamma."

LAMBERT.

Wait a moment. Here Mr. Paul, get on his back, and let Miss Sophie sit behind you. I will lead him by the halter.

SOPHIE.

But we might fall off.

LAMBERT.

There is no danger of that; I am going to

walk beside you. Moreover, he was sold to me for a perfectly gentle animal.

Lambert, aiding Paul and Sophie to mount the donkey, walked along beside them, holding him by the halter; and it was thus they reached the windows of Mme. De Réan, who, seeing them, now came out to have a good look at the donkey.

Taking him to the barn, Paul and Sophie gave him some oats, and Lambert made him a good bed of straw. The children wished to stay and see him eat; but, as it was near dinner time, they had to have their hands washed, and their hair combed, in preparation for it; so the donkey was left in company with the horses until morning.

The next day, and for some days after, he was used, harnessed to the dog-cart. Meanwhile, the order had been given for a pretty little vehicle, in which the children could go out riding, and a waggonette with which to haul dirt, flower-pots, sand,—anything that they might need for their garden. Paul learned to harness and unharness him, to rub him down, to made his bed, to feed and water him. Sophie assisted, and did almost as much as Paul himself.

Mme. De Réan bought them a pretty bridle and saddle, so that they might ride on his back. At first, the nurse used to follow them, but when every one saw that the donkey was as gentle as a lamb, Mme. De Réan allowed the children to go riding alone, forbidding them, however, to go beyond the enclosure.

One day, when Sophie was on the donkey's back, Paul tried to urge him on by touching him up with a switch.

"Don't do that, Paul;" said Sophie, "you will hurt him."

PAUL.

But he won't go, unless I give him a little of the switch ; moreover, it is so slender, it can't do him any great harm.

SOPHIE.

I have an idea! Suppose that instead of using the switch, I prick him with a spur.

PAUL.

Well, that is a funny idea! First, you have no spur ; and then his hide is so tough and thick that he wouldn't feel the spur if you had one.

SOPHIE.

Let us try it, anyhow; so much the better if it doesn't hurt him.

PAUL.

But you haven't any.

SOPHIE.

We will make one out of a big pin that we can stick in my shoe—the head inside the shoe, the point outside.

PAUL.

How ingenious that is! Have you a pin?

SOPHIE.

No, but we can return to the house and ask in the kitchen for some pins; there are always some very big ones there.

Paul mounted behind Sophie and they came up to the kitchen in a gallop. The cook gave them two pins, supposing that Sophie had torn some of her clothing. Sophie would not fix her spur before the house, for she knew very well that she was engaged in a piece of mischief, and she feared being caught in the act by her mother, who would scold her.

"It will be much better to fix it in the woods," said she; "there we can sit on the grass, and let the donkey quietly graze around us; we will look like weary travellers resting."

Reaching the woods Sophie and Paul got off the donkey, and seating themselves on the ground, began their work; the donkey meanwhile, pleased at being rid of them, amusing himself by nibbling the grass along the edge of the road.

The first pin they succeeded in getting through the leather; but it was so bent that they could not use it. Fortunately, they had another, which easily went through the shoe already pierced. Sophie now fastened it. Paul caught the donkey and assisted Sophie to mount. Pressing her heel against the poor little animal, she makes him feel the spur. He starts off in a trot. Delighted, she pricks him with it more and more; the trot changes to a gallop and his speed is such that Sophie is filled with fear. She throws herself forward and clings to his neck, her heel pressing against the animal and running the pin farther into his flesh. The tighter she clings, the deeper she pricks him; he begins to kick and jump, and, at last, throws her off, landing her about ten steps from him. She finds herself on the road, somewhat stunned by the fall. Paul who had been left behind, now comes running up very much frightened. Assisting Sophie to rise, he perceives that her nose and hands are scratched.

"Oh! what will mamma say?" she says to Paul. "What can we tell her when she asks how I happened to get thrown?"

PAUL.

We will tell her the truth, of course.

SOPHIE.

Oh! no, no, Paul; don't mention the pin.

PAUL.

And what do you wish me to say?

SOPHIE.

Say that the donkey kicked, and I fell off.

PAUL.

But he is so gentle, he would never have kicked except for that cursed pin.

In her fright she held on tight to the donkey. Page 239).

SOPHIE.

If you mention the pin, mamma will scold us and she will take the donkey from us.

PAUL.

Well, for my part, I believe it better always to tell the truth. Every time you conceal anything from aunt, she finds it out all the same, and you are punished more severely than you would have been, if you had told her the truth.

SOPHIE.

But why do you wish me to speak of the pin? It would be no lie not to mention that. I am telling the truth when I say that the donkey kicked and I fell off.

PAUL.

Do as you please about it, but I think you are wrong.

SOPHIE.

Don't you say anything, Paul; don't you mention the pin.

PAUL.

Be easy about that; you know I don't like to have you scolded.

Paul and Sophie now sought the donkey which ought to have been quite near them; but in vain, he was not to be seen. "No doubt, he has gone back to the house," said Paul.

They now turned their own faces in that direction. Reaching a little woods very near the chateau, they heard their names called and saw their mammas running,

"What has happened children?" said the latter. "Are you hurt? Your donkey came back in a gallop with his bridle broken; and he was so wild with fright that he could hardly be caught. We saw him return thus, and were much afraid some accident had befallen you."

SOPHIE.

No, mamma, none at all, only I fell off.

MME. DE RÉAN.

Fell off? how? what was the cause of it?

SOPHIE.

I was on the donkey's back, when, all of a sudden, I don't know why, he began to kick and jump. I got thrown to the ground, and my nose and hands are a little scratched but that is nothing.

MME. D'AUBERT.

Why, Paul, did he kick? I thought he was so gentle.

PAUL.

Sophie was on him, mamma, not I; it was with her he kicked.

MME. D AUBERT.

Yes, I understand; but what made him kick?

SOPHIE.

Oh! just because, aunt, he wanted to kick?

MME. D'AUBERT.

I can readily believe that it was not because he wished to be quiet. It is certainly very singular, however.

They all entered the house, just as Mme. d'Aubert finished speaking. Sophie went to her room to wash her face and hands, covered with sand, and to change her dress which was torn and dirty. Just as she (Sophie) had finished dressing, Mme. De Réan came into the room.

Examining Sophie's torn dress, she said:

"You must have had a hard fall indeed, for your dress to be so dirty and torn.

"Ugh! ugh!" cried the nurse.

MME. DE RÉAN.

What is the matter? have you hurt yourself?

THE NURSE.

Ah! what a pretty idea! Ha! ha! ha! here is an invention! Do look, Madame!

And she showed Mme. De Réan the big pin

that had just pricked her, Sophie having forgotten to remove it from the shoe, after her fall.

MME. DE RÉAN.

What does this mean? How did this pin get in your shoe, Sophie?

THE NURSE.

It certainly did not get in there of itself, for the leather is quite hard to pierce.

MME. DE RÉAN.

Speak, Sophie, and tell me how this pin got here.

SOPHIE, (*greatly embarrassed*).

I don't know, mamma, I really don't know anything about it.

MME. DE RÉAN.

What! you don't know! you put on this shoe, with the pin in it, and never saw it.

SOPHIE.

Yes, mamma, I didn't see it at all.

THE NURSE.

Ah! no, Miss Sophie, that is not true. I

put your shoes on you, and there was no pin in either of them then, I know. You would make your mamma believe that I am very careless, and that is not right, Miss.

Sophie makes no reply; she only grows more embarrassed, and her face gets a deeper crimson. Mme. De Réan commands her to speak.

"If you do not tell me the truth, Miss," says her mother, "I will ask Paul who never lies."

Sophie bursts into sobs, but she is so obstinate that she will not confess what she has done. Mme. De Réan now goes to her sister, Mme. D'Aubert, with whom she finds Paul. She asks him to tell her the meaning of that pin in Sophie's shoe. Paul seeing that his aunt is much displeased, and believing that Sophie has already told her the truth answers:

"It was for a spur, aunt."

MME. DE RÉAN.

And what did she want with a spur?

PAUL.

To make the donkey gallop.

MME. DE RÉAN.

Ah! now I understand why he kicked and threw her off. The pin pricked the poor animal, and he got rid of her as best he could.

Mme. De Réan now returned to Sophie, and said to her:

"I know it all, Miss, you are a little liar. If you had told me the truth, I should have scolded you some, but not have punished you. Now however, not for a whole month are you to mount your donkey, and this, because of the lies you have told me."

Mme. De Réan retired, leaving Sophie in tears. When Paul saw Sophie again he could not forbear saying to her:

"You see I spoke truly, Sophie, when I told you it would be better to tell the thing as it really happened. If you had done so, we should not have been deprived of our donkey, and you would not have been so distressed as you now are."

Mme. De Réan kept her word, despite Sophie's entreaties, and for one month, the children were not allowed to get on the donkey.

XX.

The Little Carriage.

SOPHIE, perceiving that her mamma could not be prevailed upon to let them ride the donkey within the prohibited time, said one day to Paul:

"Since we may not ride on our donkey's back, Paul, let us harness him to our little cart; we could take turns in driving.

PAUL.

I should wish nothing better; but would aunt permit that?

SOPHIE.

You go ask her. I dare not.

Paul ran to his aunt and asked permission to harness the donkey to their little carriage. She consented, but on condition that the nurse accompany them. When Paul mentioned this proviso, Sophie was much displeased, and grumbled a great deal.

"It is so annoying," said she, "to be bothered with the nurse all the time, wherever we go; she is always fearful of something happening; and I know she'll not let us gallop along."

PAUL.

But we must not drive at that gait anyhow, for aunt, you well know has forbidden it.

Sophie made no reply, but was very disagreeable and sulky, during the whole time that Paul was seeking the nurse and harnessing up the donkey. In about half an hour, the donkey and little carriage were at the door.

Sophie still pouting, got into the carriage; and despite all poor Paul's efforts to restore her amiability and gaiety, she continued to sulk during the whole of the ride. At last, he said to her.

"You worry me, Sophie, with your ill-humor, and I am going back to the house. It is truly annoying to look at your frowning face, as well as to have no one to speak a word to, or to play with."

And Paul turned the donkey's face homewards. Sophie said nothing, but still pouted. In alighting, she caught her foot on the step and fell. Good little Paul immediately jumped out and helped her up. She was not hurt, but Paul's kindness touched her, and she began to cry.

"Did you hurt yourself, my poor Sophie?" said he, embracing her. "Lean on me; I am not afraid, I will hold you up."

"No, dear Paul," answered Sophie, sobbing. "I am not hurt at all; I am crying because I feel sorry for having been so bad to you, who are always good and kind to me."

PAUL.

Don't cry any more for that, Sophie. I have no merit in being good to you; for I love you, and in pleasing you, I please myself, too.

Sophie threw her arms around Paul's neck, and embracing him, cried more bitterly than ever. Paul was at a loss how to console her. At last, he said:

"Listen to me, Sophie; if you keep on crying, you will make me cry, too, for it distresses me to see you so grieved."

Sophie wiped her eyes, and, amid her tears

and sobs, promised him she would cease crying.

"Oh! let me cry, Paul," she now sobbed again, "let me cry; it does me good. I begin to feel better."

When she saw Paul's eyes filled with tears, she dried her own tears, and tried to look smiling. They went together to her room, where they played until dinner.

Next day, Sophie proposed another ride in their donkey-cart. The nurse said she could not accompany them, for she had some washing to do; nor could Paul's mother or Sophie's go with them, as they were to pay a visit to Mme. De Fleurville, who lived about a league's distance.

"What are we going to do, then?" said Sophie, with a rueful countenance.

"If I felt sure that you both would be very good," said Mme. De Réan, "I should permit you to go by yourselves; but you, Sophie, are always getting up such singular ideas, that I am in constant dread of an accident from one of *these ideas.*"

SOPHIE.

Oh! no, mamma, make your mind easy! I

shall not have an *idea* this time, I assure you. Please let us two, Paul and me, go out by ourselves; the donkey is so gentle!

MME. DE RÉAN.

He is indeed gentle when not tormented; but if you attempt to spur him as you did the other day, or do anything of that sort, he will upset the little carriage.

PAUL.

Oh! no, aunt, Sophie will never repeat that trick, nor I either. I had a share in that, and deserved a scolding just as much as she did, since I helped her to stick the pin through her shoe.

MME. DE RÉAN.

Well, I will let you go alone this time; but you must not venture on the public road; keep within the enclosure, and do not drive too fast.

"Thanks, mamma, thanks, aunt," cried the two children, running immediately to the stable to harness the donkey. Just as they were about to start, there came along the farmer's two little boys, who were returning from school.

"Are you going to take a ride, Sir?" asked the elder of them, Andrew by name.

PAUL.

Yes; will you come with us?

ANDREW.

I can't leave my brother, Sir.

SOPHIE.

We'll take your brother, too.

ANDREW.

Oh! thank you, Miss, we'll be very much pleased to go with you.

SOPHIE.

Which of us is going to take the driver's seat?

PAUL.

If you drive now, here is the whip for you.

SOPHIE.

No, I prefer driving later, when the donkey is somewhat fatigued and less lively.

All four got into the little vehicle, and they drove about for two hours, sometimes in a walk, sometimes in a trot, each one taking turns in driving. The poor animal was now quite fatigued; and as he hardly felt the whip the children put to him, he went more and more slowly, despite the continued lashes and cries ("hu! hu! then!") of Sophie who was driving.

ANDREW.

Miss, if you want to make him go, let me get a holly-branch. I know if you whip him up with that, he'll go for sure.

SOPHIE.

That is a good idea, indeed; yes, we will make this lazy beast go.

She stopped; Andrew got out, and broke off a great branch of a holly-bush which was near by.

"Take care, Sophie," said Paul; "you know aunt told us not to prick the donkey, or spur him on in that way.

SOPHIE.

Do you suppose that a holly-branch will prick and hurt him like that pin did the other day? He'll hardly feel this.

PAUL.

Then why did you let Andrew break the holly-branch?

SOPHIE.

Because it is so much larger than our whip.

Saying this, Sophie applied the holly-branch to the back of the donkey, which immediately started off in a trot. Delighted at her success, she gave him a second cut, and a third, the poor beast going faster and faster at each application of the holly-branch. Sophie laughed, and the two little farm-boys, but Paul was grave and anxious, fearing something would happen, and Sophie get punished and scolded in consequence. They had now reached a long, steep hill. Sophie redoubled her blows, and the tormented animal went at full speed. She tried to stop him, but in vain, the donkey was running as fast as his legs could take him. The children screamed, but this only frightened him the more, and made him go faster. At last, high banks upset the carriage, the children were thrown out, and the donkey kept on, dragging after him the overturned vehicle until it was broken.

The carriage being very low, the children were not hurt, save some scratches on their faces and hands. Very sadly, they picked themselves up, the little farm-boys to return to the farm, Sophie and Paul to the château. Sophie was ashamed and uneasy, Paul quiet and sad. After walking along in silence for a while, Sophie said to Paul:

"Oh! I am so afraid of mamma, Paul! What will she say to me?

PAUL, (*sadly*).

When you took that holly-branch, I thought you would do some harm to the poor donkey. I should have spoken more sharply, and then perhaps you would have listened to me.

SOPHIE.

No, Paul, even if you had spoken sharply, I should not have listened to you, because I didn't think the holly could prick the donkey's thick skin enough to hurt him. But, oh! what will mamma say to me?

PAUL.

Alas! why are you so disobedient, Sophie?

If you would just listen to aunt, you would be scolded and punished much less.

SOPHIE.

I will try to correct myself of this fault; I assure you, I will try, but oh! it is so hard to obey!

PAUL.

It is much harder to be punished. I have noticed too that the things we are forbidden to do are dangerous; and that when we do them, something always happens that makes us afraid to see aunt and mamma.

SOPHIE.

Yes, that is really so. Oh! oh! mamma is coming now, don't you hear the carriage? Let us run as fast as we can, so as to get in before she sees us.

But in vain did they run, the carriage was swifter than they, and reached the entrance at the same time as themselves.

Mme. De Réan and Mm. D'Aubert were struck at the sight of the children's scratched faces and hands.

At last, they go up on a grassy bank and upset the wagon. (Page 258).

"Well!" exclaimed the former, "another accident! What has happened to you?"

SOPHIE.

Mamma, it was the donkey.

MME. DE BÉAN.

I felt sure of this in advance; and was anxious during the whole of my visit. But has the donkey gone mad? What did he do to you that you are so scratched up?

SOPHIE.

He threw us out mamma, and I think the carriage must be a little broken, for he kept on running after he had upset it.

MME. D'AUBERT.

I am sure that you did something to the poor animal to annoy or tease him.

Sophie hung her head and made no reply. Paul colored too and said nothing.

"Sophie," said her mother, "your countenance betrays what your aunt has divined. Now speak the truth, and tell us just what did happen."

Sophie hesitated an instant, and then, with

out the least prevarication, related to her mother and to her aunt, the little episode with which our readers are already acquainted.

"My dear children," said Mme. De Réan, "ever since you have had this donkey, there has been nothing but a series of accidents happening to you; and Sophie has been beset by *ideas* that lack common sense. So now, I am going to sell this miserable little animal, the cause of so much mischief."

SOPHIE AND PAUL, (*together*).

O mamma! O aunt! please don't sell him! We will never do so any more, never! never!

MME. DE RÉAN.

You may not do the same thing; but you, Sophie, will invent other foolish devices more dangerous perhaps than those you have already been guilty of.

SOPHIE.

No, mamma, I assure you, I will do nothing but what you permit me. I promise you I will be very obedient.

MME. DE RÉAN.

I will wait a few days longer, but I warn

you, that the very first time after this that you carry out one of your ideas, the donkey is sold.

The children thanked Mme. De Réan, who now asked where the little animal was. This reminded them that he had continued to run, after the carriage was upset, dragging it behind him.

Mme. De Réan sent for Lambert, recounted to him all that had happened, and told him to see what had become of the donkey. Lambert set off immediately in search of him, and returned in about an hour. The children awaited him anxiously.

"Well, Lambert, what news?" they both cried out at once.

LAMBERT.

Ah! Mr. Paul and Miss Sophie an accident has happened to your donkey.

SOPHIE AND PAUL, (*together*).

An accident! what?

LAMBERT.

It seems that the poor beast was wild with fright; he kept on running along the side of the road; the gate was open, he dashed out and across the public road just as the stage came up; the stage-driver had not time to check his horses which ran into the donkey and donkey-cart, upsetting and trampling on them; the horses fell, and the stage barely es-

caped being overturned. When the horses were helped up and unharnessed, the donkey was crushed to death; he didn't move any more than a stone.

At this, the children sent forth such cries

that their mothers and all the domestics came running to see what was the matter. Lambert again recounted the details of the donkey's death. Sophie and Paul were led away by their mammas, vainly endeavoring to console them, so deep was their distress. Sophie reproached herself for having been the cause of her donkey's death; and Paul reproached himself for not having made greater efforts to restrain her in doing what led to it. The rest of the day was passed sadly enough indeed.

For a long time afterwards, Sophie would cry whenever she saw a donkey that resembled hers. She never expressed a wish for another, and she did well in this, for her mamma would not have given it to her.

XXI.

The Tortoise.

SOPHIE loved animal pets. She had already had a *chicken*, a *squirrel*, a *cat*, a *donkey*. Her mamma would not let her have a dog, lest it go mad, which not unfrequently happens.

"What animal can I have for a pet?" said she, one day to her mother. "I should like to have one that could not hurt me, that could not run away, and that would not be hard to take care of.

MME. DE RÉAN, (*smiling*).

According to that, I know of nothing but a tortoise that would suit you.

SOPHIE.

Yes, indeed, it is the very thing! a tortoise is so gentle, and there is no danger of its running away.

MME. DE RÉAN. (*smiling*).

Even if it did try to run away you could always overtake it.

SOPHIE.

Buy me a tortoise, mamma! do buy me a tortoise.

MME. DE RÉAN.

What nonsense! I was only joking when I spoke to you of a tortoise. It is an ugly, stupid, dirty-looking, tiresome creature. I don't see how you could love anything so senseless.

SOPHIE.

Oh! please, mamma, get me one! It will be great amusement to me. I will be very good and try to deserve it.

MME. DE RÉAN.

Since you are so anxious to have such an ugly creature, I will give it to you, but on these two conditions: first, that you don't let it starve to death; and secondly, that I shall take it from you the first time you are guilty of any great fault.

SOPHIE.

I accept the conditions, mamma, I accept them. When may I have my tortoise?

MME. DE RÉAN.

You will have it day after to-morrow. This morning, I am going to write to your father in Paris to buy me one. He will send it to-morrow evening by the stage, and you will get it early, day after to-morrow.

SOPHIE.

Oh! a thousand thanks, mamma. Paul comes to-morrow, to spend a fortnight with us, and the tortoise will be a great amusement to him also.

Next day, to Sophie's joy, Paul arrived. When she told him of her expected tortoise, he laughed at her, and asked her what she would do with such a frightful looking creature.

"We will give it lettuce to eat," said she; "we will make it a bed of straw, we will take it out on the grass—we will find it a great source of amusement, I assure you."

The following day, the tortoise arrived. It was as large round as a plate, and reminded one in shape of the raised covers of dishes; its color was ugly and dirty-looking. The head and paws were not visible, it having withdrawn them.

"Oh! but it is ugly!" exclaimed Paul.

"I find it pretty enough," answered Sophie a little piqued.

PAUL, (*making fun of it*).

It has an especially pretty countenance and gracious smile.

SOPHIE.

Let us alone; you make fun of everything.

PAUL, (*in the same tone of ridicule*).

What I admire the most in it is its elegant figure, its graceful walk.

SOPHIE, (*getting angry*).

Hush, I tell you; I shall take my tortoise away, if you make fun of it.

PAUL.

Take it away, take it away, I beg of you, such a bright, clever creature as it is!

Sophie felt very much like running at Paul and slapping him, but remembering her promise and her mamma's threat, she contented herself with giving him a furious look. Wishing now to take her tortoise out on the grass, she picked it up, but it was too heavy for her and she let it fall. Paul who repented of having teased her, ran to her assistance, suggesting that they put the tortoise in a handkerchief, and carry it between them, each holding one side of the handkerchief. Sophie, frightened at the tortoise's fall accepted the proffered aid.

Smelling the fresh grass when placed upon it, the tortoise put out first its feet, then its head, and began to eat the grass, Sophie and Paul looking at it in astonishment.

"You see now," said Sophie, "that my tortoise isn't so stupid and tiresome."

"No," answered Paul, "it is not, but it is very ugly."

"Yes, I must acknowledge," said she "that it is ugly; its head is really frightful."

"And what horrible feet!" added Paul.

The children continued to amuse themselves with the tortoise, and to take care of it for about ten days, without anything extraordinary happening. It slept in a little summer house on some straw; it ate lettuce and grass and appeared happy.

One day, Sophie *had an idea*—it was to give the tortoise a bath. The weather was warm, and she thought, a bath in the pond would refresh and benefit her tortoise. Calling Paul, she opened the subject to him.

PAUL.

Bathe it? where.

SOPHIE.

In the kitchen-garden pond; the water there is so fresh and clear.

PAUL.

But I fear a bath may do it harm.

SOPHIE.

On the contrary, tortoises are very fond of bathing; it will be delighted.

PAUL.

How do you know they love to bathe? I, for my part, believe that they do not like the water.

SOPHIE.

I am sure they are very fond of the water. Don't crabs love the water? and don't oysters? These creatures are somewhat of the nature of a tortoise.

PAUL.

Well, then, suppose we try it in the pond.

Picking up the poor tortoise which was on the grass, quietly sunning itself, they took it to the pond, and plunged it therein. The moment it felt the water it stretched out its head and its feet, struggling vainly to escape its promised bath. Its sticky feet having touched Paul's and Sophie's hands, they both let go of it, and the poor creature sank instantly to the bottom of the pond.

The frightened children ran at once to the house of the gardener, and begged him to take it out. Knowing that the water was death to a tortoise, he hastened to the pond; and, as it was not deep, he waded in, after taking off his shoes and rolling up the legs of his pantaloons. He saw the tortoise struggling at the bottom of the pond, and rescued it promptly. He then put it near the fire to dry. The poor creature had withdrawn its head and its feet, and did not make the least movement. When it had been well warmed, the children wished to put it back in the sun on the grass.

"Wait, Mr. Paul and Miss Sophie," said the gardener, "I will carry it for you. It will eat very little, I imagine," he added.

"Do you think the bath has harmed it any?" asked Sophie.

THE GARDENER.

Certainly it has; the water is not good for tortoises.

PAUL.

Do you think it is going to be sick?

The gardener promptly rescues the turtle. (Page 276).

THE GARDENER.

As to its being sick, I can't say; but I believe it is going to die.

"Oh! my, oh!" exclaimed Sophie.

PAUL, (*in an undertone to Sophie*).

Don't be frightened; he doesn't know what he is talking about. He thinks tortoises are like cats and hate the water.

Reaching the lawn, the gardener gently put the tortoise on the grass, and returned to his work. From time to time, the children would look at the poor animal, but it remained motionless, its head and feet still invisible. Sophie was very anxious; Paul tried to reassure her.

"We must let it do just as it pleases," said he. "To-morrow, it will eat and walk about."

Towards night, they put it on its bed of straw, and set some fresh lettuce close by for it to eat. Next morning, when they went to see it, the lettuce was untouched.

"This is singular," said Sophie; "it generally eats during the night."

"Let us put it out on the grass," replied Paul; "perhaps it doesn't like the lettuce."

Paul, who now felt quite anxious himself, but tried to conceal it from Sophie, carefully examined the tortoise, which still never budged any more than if it had been a stone.

"Let us leave it here," said he to Sophie; "the sun will warm it, and do it good."

SOPHIE.

Do you think it is sick?

PAUL.

It seems so.

He did not add, "*I believe it is dead*," which he now began to fear.

For two days, Paul and Sophie continued to put the tortoise out on the grass, but it never moved; they always found it exactly in the same spot where they had placed it; and the lettuce they set before it in the evening, was still untouched next morning. At last, when putting it on the grass on the third day, they perceived an offensive odor from it.

"It is dead," said Paul, "it smells bad."

Distressed, and not knowing what to do, they were both standing looking at it, when Mme. De Réan came up.

"What are you doing, children, standing here motionless as statues, looking at the tortoise, which seems motionless, too, like yourselves?" she added, stooping down to take it up.

Holding it in her hands, she immediately perceived the offensive odor.

"Why, it is dead!" she exclaimed, throwing it down; "it smells bad."

PAUL.

Yes, aunt, I thought it was dead.

MME. DE RÉAN.

And what could have caused its death? It certainly could not have been hunger, as you have put it out on the grass every day. It seems singular that it should have died without any one knowing what was the matter with it.

SOPHIE.

I believe, mamma, that the bath killed it.

MME. DE RÉAN.

A bath? Who in the world ever thought of such a thing as making it take a bath?

SOPHIE, (*ashamed*).

I did, mamma; I thought tortoises liked the fresh water, and I put it in the kitchen-garden pond; it went to the bottom, and we couldn't get it out ourselves; so we had to go for the gardener to get it out for us, and thus it was a long time in the water.

MME. DE RÉAN.

Ah! that is one of your *ideas*. Since it has brought its own punishment, I have nothing to say except that you shall have no more animals pets; for you and Paul either kill them all or let them die. This tortoise must be removed. Here, Lambert, come get this creature which is dead and put it out of the way.

And this was the end of the poor tortoise, which was the last animal pet Sophie ever had. Some days after its death, she asked her mother to let her have a pair of those charming little Guinea pigs which she had seen on the farm, but Mme. De Réan refused. Sophie must needs obey, and henceforth, she and Paul who often came to spend some days with her, amused themselves without pets.

XXII.

The Departure.

"PAUL," said Sophie to him, one day, "why are aunt D'Aubert and mamma always whispering together? They both cry too, when whispering thus; do you know why?

PAUL.

No, I don't really know, but I heard mamma say to aunt the other day: "It is dreadful to think of leaving our relatives, our friends, our country;" and aunt answered: "Especially for a country like America."

SOPHIE.

Well, what does that mean?

PAUL.

I believe it means that mamma and aunt are going to America.

SOPHIE.

But that would not be dreadful at all; on the contrary, it would be delightful, I think. We will see tortoises in America.

PAUL.

And superb birds; ravens of all colors, red, orange, blue, violet, rose, and not of only a frightful black like ours.

SOPHIE.

Yes, and parrots and humming-birds, for mamma says there are many of these in America.

PAUL.

We shall see savages too, some of them black, some yellow, some red.

SOPHIE.

Oh! as to the savages, I should be afraid of them; they might eat us.

PAUL.

But we should not have to live among them; we should see them only when they happened to be walking about in the cities.

SOPHIE.

But why are we going to America? We are so comfortable and nicely fixed here.

PAUL.

Certainly we are. Our château is very near yours, and I see you very often. But we should be together all the time in America, which would be better still. Oh! that would make me love America.

SOPHIE.

There are mamma and aunt now, walking together; and they are crying. It makes me sad to see them cry..... They have taken a seat on the bench. Let us go console them.

PAUL.

But how shall we do it?

SOPHIE.

I don't know; but we can try, all the same.
The two children ran to their mothers.

"Dear mamma," said Sophie, "what makes you cry?"

MME. DE RÉAN.

Something, dear little one, troubles me. You would not understand it if I were to tell you.

SOPHIE.

Yes, indeed, mamma, I understand well enough that the thought of going to America troubles you greatly, because you think that I should be sorry to go. But, since aunt and Paul are going too, we will be very happy. And moreover, I like America, much, it is a very pretty country.

Whilst Sophie was speaking, Mme. De Réan, looked at her sister, Mme. D'Aubert with an air of astonishment, which broke into a smile, when the little girl said she liked America, a country of which she knew absolutely nothing.

MME. DE RÉAN.

Who told you we were going to America? and what makes you think it is this which grieves us?

PAUL.

Oh! it was I, aunt, who told Sophie that I heard you and my mamma speaking about going to America; and that you were both crying; but I assure you, Sophie was right in saying that we would be very happy in America, if we were together.

MME. D'AUBERT.

Yes, my dear children, you suspected the truth; we are really going.

PAUL.

Why, must we go, mamma?

MME. D'AUBERT.

Because one of our friends, M. Fichini, who lived in America has just died, and left us all his fortune. He was very rich and had no relatives. Your father and Sophie's father are obliged to go there to get possession of this fortune. Aunt and myself will accompany them, because we do not wish to be separated from them so long; yet it makes us sad to think of leaving our relations, our friends, our homes, our country.

SOPHIE.

But you are not leaving forever, are you, mamma?

MME. DE RÉAN.

Oh! no; for a year or two perhaps.

SOPHIE.

Well, mamma, don't cry any more then, if our stay is to be no longer than that. Just think of it, aunt and Paul will be with us all the time. Moreover, papa and uncle will be so pleased not to be by themselves whilst away from home.

The two mothers embraced each one, her child.

From that day they shed no tears on this subject, and Sophie said to Paul.

"You see, Paul, we did console them. I have always noticed how easily children can console their mothers."

"It is because there is so much love between them," answered Paul.

A few days after this the children went with their mothers to make a parting visit to their friends, Camille and Madeleine De Fleurville, who were much astonished at hearing of Paul's and Sophie's near departure for America.

"How long do you expect to be there?" inquired Camille.

SOPHIE.

Two years, I think. It is a long time.

PAUL

And when we get back, Sophie will be six years old, and I shall be eight.

MADELEINE.

And I, eight and Camille, nine.

SOPHIE.

How old you will be Camille—nine years!

CAMILLE.

Bring us some pretty things, some curiosities from America.

SOPHIE.

Shall I bring you a tortoise?

MADELEINE.

Oh! no! a tortoise? it is so stupid and ugly.
At this Paul could not help laughing.
" Why do you laugh, Paul?" asked Camille.

PAUL.

I laugh because Sophie who once had a tortoise got angry at me, one day, for saying of it exactly what you said just now.

CAMILLE.

And what became of this tortoise?

PAUL.

It died, after a bath that we made it take in the pond.

CAMILLE.

Poor thing! I am sorry I never saw it.

Sophie, who was somewhat sensitive about her tortoise, and did not like the subject mentioned, now proposed that they all go out in the fields to gather flowers; but Camille suggested that instead they go to the woods and pick wild strawberries. All joyfully agreed to the latter proposition. The strawberries were abundant, and the children found great delight in picking and eating them, the one act following immediately upon the other. After a pleasant stay of two hours, the little friends must part. Paul promised to bring back from America, fruits, flowers, humming-birds, parrots; and Sophie, promised even a little savage, if she could buy one. For the next few days, they continued their parting visits, and then came the packing up. M. De Réan and M. D'Aubert were already in Paris, awaiting the arrival of their wives and children.

The day of departure was a sad one. Even Sophie and Paul wept on leaving the château, the domestics, the village people.

"Perhaps," thought the children, "we shall never see them any more."

These poor people had the same thought, and every one was very sad.

The mammas and children got into a carriage drawn by four post-horses; the nurses and waiting-maids followed in an open, three-horse vehicle, a servant to each seat. Stopping on the road an hour for breakfast, they reached Paris in time for dinner. Here, they were to remain a week, for the purpose of making the necessary purchases for their voyage, and also for they stay in America.

This was a most delightful week to the children. They went with their mammas to the Bois de Boulogne, the Tuileries the Jardin des Plantes and they accompanied them on their shopping expeditions, to buy all sorts of things—dresses, hats, shoes, gloves, story books toys, and edibles to have in their state-rooms. Sophie was anxious to have every animal she saw for sale, even asking her mamma to buy the little giraffe at the Jardin des Plantes; and Paul wanted all the books and pictures. Each was given a nice new little travelling bag in which to carry their toilet articles, their lunches, and the games, such as dominoes, cards, marbles, etc.

At last, dawned the much desired day of their departure for Havre, the city where they were to board the ship which would take them to America. On reaching Havre they learned that their ship, La Sibylle, would not sail for three days, and these three days, they turned to account in trying to see what they could of the city. The children were highly entertained by the noise and bustle in the streets, the sight of the docks filled with shipping, the wharves covered with merchants, and their goods—parrots, monkeys and all sorts of things from America. Mme. De Réan, had she listened to Sophie, would have bought half a score of monkeys, and as many each of parrots, parroquets, little birds, tortoises. But she was firm in refusing, notwithstanding Sophie's entreaties.

These three days passed as had the week in Paris, the four years of Sophie's life, the six years of Paul's—they passed away never to return. Mme. De Réan and Mme. D'Aubert wept at leaving, even for a while, their dear and beautiful France. M. De Réan and M. D'Aubert were sad themselves, but tried to console their wives by promising to bring them back as soon as circumstances would allow. Paul and Sophie, however, were delighted, their only grief being that of seeing their mammas in tears. They all went on board the ship which, amid the storms and dangers of the deep, was to carry them to a distant land. Some hours later, they were ensconced in their cabins, pretty little chambers, just large enough to contain each, two beds, their trunks, and the necessary toilet furniture. Sophie slept with her mother, Paul with his, and the two papas together. They all ate at the table of the Captain, who became very fond of Sophie, as she recalled to him his little Marguerite in France; and he often played with Sophie and Paul. He also took pains to explain to them whatever seemed to astonish them about the ship—how it moved over the surface of the water, how it was aided to advance by the sails being unfurled,—and many other things.

Paul would say:

"I am going to be a sailor when I grow up and sail with the Captain."

"Indeed you are not, "Sophie would answer; "you are to live always with me."

PAUL.

Why can't you come with me on the Captain's ship?

SOPHIE.

Because I will not leave mamma; I am going to stay with her always, and you are to stay with me, do you hear?

PAUL.

I hear, I hear. I will stay with you since you wish it.

The voyage was long, and lasted many days. I must now say to my readers that if they wish to know more of Sophie, they must ask their mammas to read them "*Model Little Girls:*" it is here they will find her. If desirous of resuming their acquaintance with Paul, seek him in "*The Vacations,*" for it is in that book, they will be introduced to him anew.

THE END.

www.ingramcontent.com/pod-product-compliance
Lightning Source LLC
Chambersburg PA
CBHW032054220426
43664CB00008B/990